SERENDIPITY YOUTH BIBLE STUDY SERIES

Leader's Guide

SERENDIPITY YOUTH BIBLE STUDY SERIES

Leader's Guide

by
Lyman Coleman and Denny Rydberg

Scripture Union
130 City Road London EC1V 2NJ

Serendipity
YOUTH BIBLE STUDY
SERIES

Serendipity House, Box 1012, Littleton, Co 80160
USA

© 1982 Serendipity House

UK Edition © Scripture Union 1983

Published by Scripture Union,
130, City Road, London EC1V 2NJ

ISBN 0 86201 169 8

ACKNOWLEDGEMENTS
□ Joe Narracci and Cheryl Guth for a lot of the preliminary
research. □ Steve Hoke (Seattle Pacific University) and Paul
Evans and his staff (Youth Dynamics of Anacortes, Washington)
for help in writing/testing the material. □ Wayne Rice, Denny
Rydberg and Mike Yaconelli for permission to use crowd
breakers from 'Fun and Games.' © 1977 by Youth Specialties.
Used by permission from Zondervan Publishing House. □ The
American Bible Society for permission to use the Good News
Bible. © 1976, American Bible Society. □ New York International
Bible Society for permission to use the New International
Version of the Bible. © 1973, 1978, by the New York
International Bible Society.

Phototypeset by Input Typesetting Ltd., London SW19 8DR
Printed in Great Britain by
Ebenezer Baylis & Son Limited,
The Trinity Press, Worcester, and London

GENERAL INTRODUCTION

This book provides you with some guidance in the use of the three study books produced for teenagers: *Starters: On Becoming a Christian; Knowing me: On My Identity; X-Certificate: On Moral Questions.*

The Serendipity Approach

'Serendipity' is the name given to the Bible Study method used in the youth series. It means 'one surprise after another'. It is hoped that as teenagers are encouraged to use the Bible in this way they will be surprised by what they learn from each other and from God.

Each of these three student books contains seven group studies which, ideally, are used consecutively as a means of developing the life of the group. If this is not possible, leaders will be able to develop their own programme from a selection of studies.

In each study the Bible passage is printed in the booklet. The study material should help students to relate their own experiences and situation to what the Bible teaches, and so help to develop caring, supportive relationships amongst group members—a mark of true fellowship.

The Use of C-Groups

An important part of this course is that it encourages the use of C-Groups. These are small, caring units of 4–7 teenagers, plus a member of the Youth Worker Team (YWT). By using the Serendipity Bible Study material, members of C-Groups are encouraged to get to know one another, to 'share their story' (what is happening to them), to be affirmed by one another, to talk about their hopes, dreams, concerns and pains and, finally, to agree together to help one another—a key to Christian growth.

It may mean that your youth group should be subdivided into two or three smaller C-Groups. This is the ideal, but your situation may demand flexibility.

The Programme

Each Bible study is divided into three sections:

Warm-Up:	Encouraging participation and some initial thinking about the topic of study
Starter Bible Study:	Study of the Bible passage itself, relating it to life
Going Further:	Consolidating learning, and deciding on action

The Training Course

A six-session training course is available in booklet form for any adults and older teenagers who wish to develop their skills in working with young people. This course is available as a separate booklet.

STARTERS:

On Becoming a Christian

> 'But the seed on good soil stands for those with a
> noble and good heart, who hear the word, retain it,
> and by persevering produce a good crop.'
>   **LUKE 8:15, NIV**

CONTENTS

STARTERS:

WARM-UP

to build trust and
confidence in the
C-Groups before
the Bible Study

STARTER
BIBLE STUDY

to share 'my own
story' in the
C-Groups through
a Bible story

GOING
FURTHER

to go deeper into the
Bible

---

1 BEGINNINGS

Tag Me
Make a name tag from
coloured paper and
magazines that best
represents you. Then, get
together in a small group
and 'show and tell' your
masterpiece.

The Seed and the Soils
Jesus' parable of the sower
becomes the story in which
you talk about your past
growth experiences and
how ready you are to grow
now.

An Event and a Process
How does this relationship
with Christ begin? What
does the Bible say about
salvation as an event and a
process? Develop a plan for
progress.

---

2 TURNING POINT

People Bingo
Get new information from
people in your group and
apply it to your bingo card.
Can he wiggle his ears?
Did she once dye her hair?
Does he still have his
tonsils?

Who Is That Man?
Peter tells Jesus who he is
and Jesus tells the disciples
what he expects from
them. You say who you
think Jesus is and what
you think being a follower
of his demands.

Sold Out
Compare your priorities
with the biblical idea of
total commitment. Write a
note to God about your
commitment to him and
where you're finding it
hard to trust him.

---

3 GROWING PAINS

My Scrapbook
Put together an imaginary
scrapbook of favourite
eating places, holiday
places, strangest things
that ever happened to you.
Share four of these
'favourites' or 'strangests'
with your partner.

The Good Gardener
Learn about growing fruit
and find out what it has to
do with the Christian life.
Figure out how God
'gardens' in your life. What
does God need to do to
make you more 'fruitful'?
What are the benefits to
'remaining' with him?

**Love Talks, Listens,
Pleases**
Christianity is not a
religion; it's a relationship.
How do you build
relationships? Discover
how to talk to, listen to,
and please God.

On Becoming a Christian

4 STRUGGLING

Funny Faces
Think about yourself, your family, your friendships, your school, your C-Group, your God, and your church, and ask, 'How am I feeling?'

Peter's Ups and Downs
Peter (the Rock) lived a roller-coaster existence for the three years he walked on this earth with Jesus. Use Peter's life to examine your own.

About Me ... My Ups and Downs
Look at Paul instead of Peter and see what he has to say about *your* ups and downs.

5 BELONGING

Strength Bombardment
Let the members of your C-Group bombard you with your strengths. Blast them with a few of theirs.

The Mark of the Disciple
Jesus tells his disciples to love one another. What does that mean? How does it feel? Jesus tells you to do the same. What difference does it make in your life?

Personal Inventory
Reflection time. A chance to ask, 'How am I doing?' with such characteristics as compassion, consistency, honesty, humility, forgiveness and love.

6 HANGING IN THERE

Four Facts/One Lie
Give four honest statements about yourself and one lie . . . and see if the others in your C-Group can guess which statement is the lie.

Peter Bails Out
Our good friend Peter makes a major mistake. With Peter's mistake in full view, we look at a few of our own and discover how God can make failures into something good.

God's Forgiveness and Me
More on the important subject of forgiveness. What are the limits of God's forgiveness? When can't he forgive me? How am I doing in the forgiveness department?

7 NEXT STEP

Advertising Slogans
Give out some much deserved praise to those in your group that made a contribution to your life and your group during this course by giving them a slogan.

The Go-For-It Bereans
Using the story of a group of people encountered by Paul and Silas, determine the next steps you need to take. Are you ready to grow on your way?

Evaluation Exercises
What's happened in the past seven weeks? Go back and retake the relationship test and the 'soil' test from Session 1. See where you have grown.

Session 1
Beginnings

Objectives: To get better acquainted with one another; to form C-Groups for the first time in the course; to help all members of the group realise that they are special and that they are important to the group; to help members realise that growth and maturity in the Christian life are affected by how well they respond to God's Word; to evaluate how well each person receives God's Word and how they could be more responsive.

Setting: Casual, informal atmosphere—movable chairs or a rug on the floor—where the C-Groups can gather, have fun, and be relaxed.

Time: From 50 minutes to 2½ hours

- ☐ Meal/40 Minutes*
- ☐ Crowd Breakers/30 Minutes*
- ☐ C-Group Warm-Up/15 Minutes
- ☐ Starter Bible Study/40 Minutes
- ☐ Going Further/30 Minutes*

*Optional

If you have only 50 minutes, move to the C-Group Warm-Up immediately. If you have 2½ hours, the Further study can be incorporated into the regular meeting time. If not, you can assign this as homework for those interested in pursuing the subject further. For an older, or more mature group, you can condense the time required for the Starter Bible Study and spend more time on the Further study as a group.

Materials required:

- ☐ Student Books
- ☐ Pens
- ☐ Paper, magazines, glue, scissors, string or wool, crayons or felt pens.
- ☐ Equipment for Crowd Breakers

Leadership: Study the 'Leaders' Checklist'.

Meal: If you are planning on a meal make sure you've contacted a mum or dad to prepare the meal. Ask the group to bring the amount of money necessary to cover the cost, and hand this on to the parents providing the meal. Invest in some paper napkins, plates, cups—to reduce the amount of washing-up.

Crowd Breakers: To start off the meeting choose one or two mixers/crowd breakers. Some of the crowd breakers are for the whole group and some are for small-group/C-Groups after they have been formed. Note the extra materials that are needed for each crowd breaker. It is an excellent way for team members to get acquainted.

**INTRODUCTION
All Together/3
Minutes**

Welcome

Welcome the group and introduce them to this session. SAY something like: 'I want to welcome each one of you here. For the next

7 weeks, we're going to be involved in a course called "Starters," which deals with what it means to become a Christian and to grow in that relationship with Jesus Christ. (DISTRIBUTE the Student Books and pens.) Open your booklet to the 'contents' table in the front. I'd like to review some of the topics we'll be covering.'

GIVE them a brief overview, quickly touching on the topics: Beginnings, Turning Point, Growing Pains, etc., without going into much detail. After you've finished the quick review, continue by SAYING something like: 'After the meal and/or a few games each week, we'll break into small groups called C-Groups. Each C-Group will consist of from 4 to 6 students (save some room for newcomers) and one leader. The C-Group leaders for this course will be: (READ off the names of the people you and the Youth Worker Team have put together for the C-Groups. Make sure you have places for one or two new members in each C-Group.)

ASK them to join their C-Group leaders as you read their names. As soon as they've grouped, MOVE to one of the crowd breakers for C-Groups or the Warm-Up below.

WARM-UP C-Groups/15 Minutes

Tag Me

Step 1; 5 Minutes. ASK each person to turn to Session 1 in their booklets and read the directions on 'Tag Me.' DEMONSTRATE what you mean by showing your own 'name tag' and explaining the various tear-outs that describe you.

GIVE each C-Group a stack of coloured paper, magazines, glue, and enough string or wool for each person to wear their name tag like a medallion around their neck.

ENCOURAGE them to be creative. Tell them to work quickly—tearing out pictures, words, slogans, etc., from the magazine and making their name tag. GIVE them 5 minutes to complete their tag.

Step 2; 5 Minutes. When the name tags have been completed, tell them to regather in C-Groups and explain their 'masterpiece' to their C-Group. Ask the C-Group leader to go first. Then, give each person about 30 seconds to explain his or her name tag.

(Leader's Note: Make sure there's plenty of every material—magazines, newspapers, glue, etc.—so people don't have to wait long to put the tag together. This is *not* an artistic exercise. It is a fun way to introduce yourself with a 'show and tell' name tag. The enthusiasm of the Group leaders should be infectious.)

Step 3; 5 Minutes. Then ASK each person to turn to the diagram of the cricket pitch and SAY something like: 'To begin this course, I'd like all of us to decide where we are right now with God and with this group. The diagram of the cricket pitch gives you several "places" to indicate where you might be in these two relationships.'

READ the directions carefully and SHOW where you would put the two symbols. (Pause 1 minute while everyone places the two symbols.) Now, REGATHER with your C-Group and explain where you placed the symbols and why. C-Group leaders 'go first' and set an example of honesty and openness. . . . POINT OUT that it is okay to be anywhere on the diagram. The C-Group leader should give 'permission' for anyone to say they are in 'outfield' if that is where they are.

STARTER BIBLE STUDY
C-Groups/35–40 Minutes

The Seed and the Soils

SAY something like: 'Now let's begin with the first session.'

(In advance, SELECT a student who is a good reader and who would be happy to read the Bible passage. When you have him/her read, let the group know that you selected him/her several days ago so that the others will have no anxiety that they will be called on to read at any moment. Many teenagers are not confident of their reading ability and are in fear of being called upon to read aloud. Don't let them sense a threat here.)

(Preparation, 7 Minutes) After the passage has been read, ASK C-Groups to form pairs and work together on the first part of the questionnaire, 'Looking into the Story.' If there is an odd number, ask the C-Group leader to take one person or form a group of three. Allow about 7 minutes for partners to work on the Bible story questions.

(Discussion, 5–7 Minutes) When it looks like most people are finished, REGATHER as C-Groups and DISCUSS the questions. (Make sure they understand the difference in the soils.) As part of the discussion, ASK them how the farmer would feel about the different kinds of soils.

(Preparation, 5–7 Minutes) Then INSTRUCT each person to work alone (solo) on the 'My Own Story'

section. Allow about 5–7 minutes for these questions.

(Discussion, 15–20 Minutes) REGATHER as C-Groups again and DISCUSS the 'My Own Story' questions. Read the first question and go around your group. Then, around again on question 2, etc. Be careful not to drag information from those who don't want to volunteer it. This is the first of 7 studies and as the group becomes better acquainted, people will share spontaneously.

In the discussion, UNDERLINE the fact that growth in our life will only occur when we really allow God's Word to take root and grow—only when we're receptive to what God wants to teach us. SPEND some time discussing these things that keep us from being good soil.

CLOSE in prayer in C-Groups. Thank God especially for each member of your group.

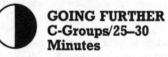

GOING FURTHER
C-Groups/25–30 Minutes

An Event and a Process

If you have time, ask your Group to work, in pairs again, on all of the questions in the Further study, except those in the Personal Application. If you don't have time, ask them to work on the section at home. The point is to help everyone understand what salvation is, and how to find it, that it begins with an event—receiving and believing what God gives—and continues as a process—growth.

A discussion of these questions provides an excellent opportunity to discover how many of the members of your C-Group are Christians and how many are in the process of becoming.

Optional Crowd Breakers

LET'S GET ACQUAINTED
The following list should be copied out and given to each person in the group. The idea is to fill in each blank on your sheet with someone who fits the description. The first person to get all his blanks filled, or the one who has the most at the end of the time limit is the winner. The sample list below is only a suggested list. Be creative and come up with your own. This is a good way for people to get to know each other a little better.

Find someone who uses 'Crest' toothpaste
Find someone who has two bathrooms in his house
Find someone who has red hair
Find someone who gets shouted at for slurping coffee
Find someone who has been in the cockpit of an aeroplane
Find someone who plays a guitar
Find someone who likes Chinese food
Find someone who has been to the Channel Islands
Find someone who uses your brand of toothpaste
Find a girl who wears contact lenses
Find a guy who has been skiing
Find someone who knows what 'charisma' means
Find someone who is on a diet
Find someone (boy or girl) who uses an electric shaver
Find someone with a bunch of keys
Find someone who doesn't like bananas
Find someone who didn't know your surname
Find someone who is good at climbing trees

(See Session 2 for more crowd breakers.)

LEADERS' CHECKLIST

BEFORE THE SESSION
☐ Student Books and pens. Make sure you have enough.

☐ C-Groups Leaders: Qualified group leaders for every 4 to 6 teenagers, who have completed the 6 training sessions.

☐ Meal: Get one of the parents to prepare spaghetti or something else cheap and simple.

☐ Crowd Breakers: Pick one or two from the box.

☐ Room: Select a room that is large enough for the group games—with a cosy corner for C-Groups.

☐ Name Tags: Create one or two samples to 'show and tell.'

DURING THE SESSION

☐ C-Groups: The objective of this session is to establish C-Groups. Divide the total group into smaller Groups of 4–6 and place one leader from the Youth Worker Team in each C-Group.

☐ Student Books: Pass out books to everyone. Write names in the front.

☐ Partners: Split into pairs within the C-Groups to work on the Starter Bible Study. Then, regather in C-Groups for discussion.

AFTER THE SESSION

☐ Collect: Collect the Student Books unless you are assigning the Further Study as homework.

☐ C-Groups: Get together with your C-Group leaders. Evaluate the session and assign people to lead the crowd breakers at the next session—collect the necessary supplies.

☐ Order: Order more Student Books for newcomers.

Session 2
Turning Point

Objectives: To get better acquainted in C-Groups, to discover the type of commitment God wants us to have with him, to learn what it means to 'take up your cross, deny self, and follow me,' to trust God in the hard areas of life where we are sometimes afraid to trust him, and to realise that Christianity is a relationship not a religion and that this relationship with Jesus is a joyous one.

Setting: Adequate for the large-group crowd breakers and the small-group sharing.

Time: From 50 minutes to 2½ hours
- ☐ Meal/40 Minutes*
- ☐ Crowd Breakers/30 Minutes*
- ☐ C-Group Warm-Ups/8–10 Minutes
- ☐ Starter Bible Study/35–40 Minutes
- ☐ Going Further/25–30 Minutes*
*Optional

If you have only 50 minutes, move to the C-Group Warm-Up immediately. If you have 2½ hours, the Further Study can be incorporated into the regular meeting time. If not, you can assign this as homework for those interested in pursuing the subject further. For an older, or more mature group, you can condense the time required for the Starter Bible Study and spend more time on the Further Study.

Materials required:
- ☐ Student Books
- ☐ Pens
- ☐ Equipment for Crowd Breakers

Leadership: Note the 'Leaders' Checklist'.

WITH THIS STUDY, BE ESPECIALLY CAREFUL NOT TO LAY ANY ADDITIONAL BURDEN ON THE GROUP. Help them to realise that although the demands are heavy, the burden is light . . . that it is exciting and joyful to be a committed Christian. Let them see that dynamic in your lives.

Meal: If you are planning a meal, make sure you've contacted a mum or dad for the food and have told everyone how much money they need to bring to cover the cost.

Crowd Breakers: Select one or two of the crowd breakers over the page to start off the meeting. Some are for the entire group and some are for the C-Groups.

Review: If you assigned the Further Study as a take-home assignment last week, take a few moments and ask how it went.

WARM-UP
All together/8–10 Minutes

People Bingo

WELCOME the group and DISTRIBUTE the Student Books. ASK them to turn to Session 2, where they will see the People Bingo sheet.

READ the instructions and EXPLAIN: 'You can ask anyone *two* questions and this person can ask you *two* questions before you move on to another person. (*Leader: If you have a small youth group you may allow them to return to the same person twice.*) If the answer is "yes" to any question, jot down their first name in the box. The first person to fill in all the boxes on the card wins. You can approach ANYONE in the room.' TURN them loose.

When you have a winner, ASK for their bingo card and read aloud the names on this person's card for each box. ASK these people to confirm if this is so. Then, move into the C-Groups for the Starter Bible Study.

STARTER BIBLE STUDY
C-Groups/35–40 Minutes

Who Is That Man?

SELECT someone in advance to read the Bible passage.

(*Preparation, 7–10 Minutes*) After the Bible passage has been read, ASK the C-Groups to divide into twos and work together on the questions in 'Looking into the Story.' Then let them finish the questions in 'My Own Story' on their own.

(*Discussion, 10 Minutes*) REGATHER by C-Groups and DISCUSS the questions under 'Looking into the Story.' Concentrate on questions 3 to 7. Help the students gain an understanding of what it means to 'deny self, take up the cross daily, and follow Christ.'

(*Preparation/Discussion, 20 Minutes*) MOVE on to the 'My Own Story' questions. Some of the answers for

2 and 3 may seem as if they were written to provide comic relief, but they could be real options in the lives of some of the group, like 'being seen with my parents in public.' Some teenagers hate to be seen with their parents, but it might be a way God is calling them to honour their parents. As you move through the discussion, help them to learn that: (1) God calls us to *total* commitment, (2) this commitment involves a change in our actions and attitudes right where we live (following Jesus is very practical), but (3) Christianity is not drudgery or joyless. Convey to them in the midst of these 'hard verses' that there is joy in following Jesus; that Christianity is not a religion; it is a relationship; and it's the greatest relationship they'll ever have. Give them a sense of the joy that you experience in your life.

CLOSE in prayer in the C-Groups, thanking Jesus for his call to commitment and asking him to help everyone in the C-Group to understand better what it means to have a relationship with him.

GOING FURTHER
C-Groups/25–30 Minutes

Sold Out

If you have time, have the partners get together again and work on the questions in the Further Study. If partners feel like sharing their prayers with one another, they can. Otherwise, the prayers are personal.

REGATHER the C-Group and DISCUSS the questions. ASK if anyone wants to share anything about their prayers in the Personal Application. If they don't, don't try to get discussion.

Optional Crowd Breakers

PASS THE BALLOON

Give each C-Group a large balloon. When the whistle blows, start passing the balloon around the group. When the whistle blows again, whoever is holding the balloon gets a penalty:

☐ First penalty: you must stand up and sit down before you can pass the balloon.

☐ Second penalty: you must stand up and turn around before you can pass the balloon.

☐ Third penalty: you must stand up, turn around, laugh like a hyena, flap your arms like a bird, and sit down before you can pass the balloon.

Pass out a balloon to each group. When the whistle blows, start passing the balloon. When the whistle blows again, the person holding the balloon is penalised. Keep track of your penalties.
(Leader: vary the time between whistles to add tension and excitement.)

RHYTHM *(For C-Groups to work on as teamwork)*

Everyone in the room numbers off in a circle (1, 2, 3, 4 etc.) with 'number 1' in the end chair. The 'rhythm' is begun by number 1 and everyone joins in by first slapping thighs, clapping hands, then snapping right-hand fingers, then snapping left-hand fingers in a continuous 1–2–3–4–1–2–3–4–1–2–3–4, motion, at a moderately slow speed. (It may speed up after everyone learns how to play.) The real action begins when number 1, on the first snap of the fingers, calls out his own number, and on the second snap of the fingers, calls somebody else's number. For example, it might sound something like this: (slap) (clap) 'ONE, SIX!' and then the person who is number 6 (as an example) might go: (slap) (clap) 'SIX, TEN!' and then number ten would do the same thing, calling out someone else's number on the second finger snap, and so on. If anyone misses, he goes to the end and everyone who was after him before moves up one number. The object is to arrive eventually at the number one chair.

BALLOON POP RELAY *(For two or three teams)*

Divide your group into teams. The teams line up single file at a starting line. A chair is placed about 30 feet away. Each team member has a deflated balloon. One at a time, the team members run to the chair, blow up their balloon, tie it, pop it by sitting on it, and go to the end of the team line. First team to pop all of its balloons wins.

THREAD THE NEEDLE *(For two teams)*

For this game you will need two blunt table knives (the old-fashioned kind that had a 'neck' between the blade and the handle) and two balls of string (medium weight).

Divide the group into two teams. The teams start exactly the same time to . . . 'thread the needle' (the knife with the end of the string tied tightly to the neck of the knife) down through their shirt and one trouser leg (or . . . their blouse and skirt or shorts etc.). This person then passes the 'needle' on to the person behind him to do the same and on down to the end of the line. Each team member is constantly busy, for he is continually feeding 'thread' (the string) along the way, so that there is enough thread to connect the entire team.

When the last person has 'threaded the needle,' he then begins the process of 'unthreading the needle'! This is done by pulling up on the string and getting the 'needle' (knife) up, through, and out of his slacks and shirt (or whatever!). This takes constant teamwork, for when 'unthreading the needle,' each team member works to pass the slack in the string along so, at the end, the first person in line has the string in a neat ball again. And the team has been able to complete the whole procedure without the 'thread' becoming detached from the 'needle' at any given time!

The fun part of the game is to try in every way to make it a speedy relay. The fun mounts as members help team-mates along yet keeping the 'thread' from getting knotted, the 'needle' from getting stuck, etc.

This game has proved to be an excellent, exciting game for all age groups, from young teenage girls and boys, to adults.

LEADERS' CHECKLIST
BEFORE THE SESSION

- ☐ Student Books: Do you have enough?

- ☐ C-Groups: Ask the C-Group leaders to contact their Group members during the week.

- ☐ Meal: Ask a parent to prepare an inexpensive, hot meal. Charge everyone enough to cover the cost.

- ☐ Crowd Breakers: Choose one or two games to start off the session. Some are for the whole group and some are for C-Groups. Do you have the equipment?

- ☐ Team: Continue your training of the Youth Worker Team. (The course is contained in a separate Serendipity publication, *Six Training Sessions for your Youth Worker Team.)*

DURING THE SESSION

- ☐ Welcome: Welcome newcomers. Give out Student Books. Write their names in the front. Place newcomers in existing C-Groups.

- ☐ Warm up: The entire group stays together.

- ☐ C-Groups: Within C-Groups, work in pairs on the questionnaire before getting together for sharing as a C-Group.

AFTER THE SESSION

- ☐ Collect: Collect the Student Books unless you are assigning the Further study for homework.

- ☐ Order: Order more Student Books for newcomers.

- ☐ Team meeting: Get together with C-Group leaders/Youth Workers and (1) evaluate the session, (2) go over the next session lesson plan, (3) assign people to lead the crowd breakers, and (4) plan a weekend or day away at the end of the course.

Session 3
Growing Pains

Objectives: To build greater trust and confidence within C-Groups, to discover the source of spiritual growth and what the 'good gardener' does in our lives, and to determine to 'remain in him.'

Setting: Plenty of room for crowd breakers and a cosy area for the C-Groups to relax and share.

Time: From 50 minutes to 2½ hours
- Meal/40 Minutes*
- Crowd Breakers/30 Minutes*
- C-Group Warm-Up/10–15 Minutes
- Starter Bible Study/35–40 Minutes
- Going Further/25–30 Minutes*

*Optional

If you have only 50 minutes, move to the C-Group Warm-Up immediately. If you have 2½ hours, the Further Study can be incorporated into the regular meeting time. If not, you can assign this as homework for those interested in pursuing the subject further. For an older, or more mature group, you can condense the time required for the Starter Bible Study and spend more time on the Further Study.

Materials required:

- Student Books
- Pens
- Equipment for Crowd Breakers

Leadership: Check the 'Leaders' Checklist'.

Meal: If you are planning on a meal, make sure you've contacted a mum or dad for the hot meal and that you've told everyone how much money they need to bring.

Crowd Breakers: Select one or two from the special box. Some are for the whole group and some are for small C-Groups.

Review: If you assigned the Further Study as homework in session 2, you may want to ask about it before you move to the C-Group Warm-Up. Assess your time and plan your schedule accordingly if you wish to add the discussion of the Further Study to the time schedule.

WARM-UP
C-Groups/10–15
Minutes

My Scrapbook

WELCOME the group.
DISTRIBUTE the Student Books. (Ask any newcomers to put their names inside.) ASK them to turn to Session 3.
READ the directions in the Student Book carefully and EXPLAIN what you would write or draw in two or three boxes. ASK everyone to think about the squares and fill in the *first thing that comes to mind* for each square. GIVE them 3 or 4 minutes in silence.

Then, GATHER in C-Groups and ASK each person to take 1 minute to explain their scrapbook to their C-Group.

STARTER BIBLE STUDY
C-Groups/35–40 Minutes

The Good Gardener

(Leader's Note: This Starter Bible Study is filled with more content questions than usual. You will have to keep the pace moving—without displaying 'agenda anxiety'—but it is worth the effort. They will discover much about growth.)

SELECT someone in advance to read the text and have him/her read it.

(Preparation, 8–10 Minutes) ASK the C-Groups to split up into groups of 2 and work with a partner on the 'Looking into the Story' questions.

(Discussion, 8–10 Minutes) REGATHER in C-Groups and SHARE the answers to 'Looking into the Story.' CONCENTRATE on questions 5 to 8. Make it your aim to help the Group develop a 'garden mentality'. HELP them to understand what the terms 'remain . . . prune . . . fruit,' etc., mean. This is very necessary before they move to the next section.

(Preparation, 8–10 Minutes) MOVE ON to the questions under 'My Own Story' and ask everyone to answer the questions on their own. (Leader: these questions are a little more difficult than the ones the students experienced in the first two sessions. So, CIRCULATE around, encouraging those who may be having some trouble, helping those who need a little help.)

(Discussion, 8–10 Minutes) CALL the C-Groups back together. SPEND the rest of the time in discussion. Begin with question 1 and go around. Give equal time to the questions. Some points to emphasise:

☐ good growth comes from God

☐ we must 'remain in him' to grow

☐ all of us *will* have growing pains

☐ God, the gardener, prunes those whom he loves

☐ there are some fantastic benefits to being in God's garden

ENCOURAGE each student to really make a commitment to 'remain in Christ.'

CLOSE in prayer in C-Groups, praying for the person on your right.

Optional Crowd Breakers

COMMUNICATION (*For C-Groups to build communication*)
Divide into C-Groups. Station one half of each C-Group at opposite ends of the room. On the word GO, one person from each C-Group is given an envelope with a message in it. This person opens the envelope, reads the message, screws it up, and throws it away. This person then *runs* to the next person (opposite end of room) and whispers the message. Then the second person runs back to the next person and whispers the message and so on until the last person runs to the 'referee' and whispers it to him. The team closest to the original message wins. Accuracy, not time, is most important, but they must run. Sample message: 'Mrs. Sarah Sahara sells extraordinary information to very enterprising executives.'

FINGERS UP
Get into pairs. Put hands behind your back. On the word GO, everyone brings his hands out in front of him with any number of fingers up. The first person to call out the correct total number of 'fingers up'—combining your fingers and your partner's fingers—wins. Repeat three or four times.

ITALIAN KARATE
The same as Fingers Up except each person puts just *one* hand behind his back and brings out *one* hand with any number of fingers up WHILE calling out a number from 1 to 10. Then, if your fingers and your partner's fingers add up to this number, you win.

Again, you call out a number from 1 to 10 *as you bring out your fingers*. You do not wait to see or count the fingers. On the word GO, call out a number and bring out your fingers at the same time. Repeat several times . . . until someone wins.

FLAMINGO FOOTBALL
Announce that you are going to play 'rugby, boys against the girls!' The guys usually get pretty charged up about that idea. Then announce that the rules are the same as regular rugby, except for one thing. The boys must hold one foot up off the ground with one hand at all times. They must run, pass, catch, and even kick on one foot. The girls usually clobber the guys with this one.

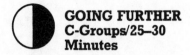

GOING FURTHER
C-Groups/25–30 Minutes

Love Talks, Listens, and Pleases

If you have time, let the partners get together again and work on the Further Study—except for the Personal Application.

REGROUP and DISCUSS the questions, helping the group understand how God speaks and how they can listen. Then have group members (unless they are reluctant to do so) share what their Personal Application points are. Suggest that the partners phone each other in the middle of the week to see how the application is going.

LEADERS' CHECKLIST

BEFORE THE SESSION

☐ Student Books: Do you have enough for newcomers?

☐ Meal: Is someone preparing the food?

☐ Absentees: Ask C-Group leaders to contact anyone who was absent from their group at the last meeting.

☐ Team Training: Go over the lesson plan with your C-Group leaders.

☐ Research: Check a Bible Dictionary for 'vine' or 'pruning'—to get some background to the Bible passage.

DURING THE SESSION

☐ Welcome: Welcome newcomers. Give them books. Write their names inside. Assign to a C-Group before the Warm-Up.

☐ Modelling: C-Group leaders 'go first' on the scrapbook exercise and set the pace for openness and honesty.

☐ Partners: Inside C-Groups, work on the Bible study in pairs before getting back together for discussion.

AFTER THE SESSION

☐ Collect: Collect the books.

☐ Crowd Breakers: Assign people on YWT to collect the equipment for crowd breakers next time.

☐ Reorder: Order more Student Books.

☐ Team Training: Get together with Youth Worker Team for personal support and strategy planning. Think further about overnight retreat. It doesn't have to be elaborate. Just a night in the church hall or someone's house, with a trip out the following day, would be fine.

Session 4
Struggling

Objectives: To get closer in the C-Groups; to realise that one of the 'biggies' of the faith, Peter, had ups and downs; to analyse what gives us our ups and downs in life; to discover how God helps us overcome our downs; to continue to build a learning, caring, sharing community.

Setting: Casual—with plenty of room for the crowd breakers and a cosy corner for settling down in C-Groups.

Time: From 50 minutes to 2½ hours

☐ Meal/40 Minutes*
☐ Crowd Breakers/30 Minutes*
☐ C-Group Warm-Up/8–10 Minutes
☐ Starter Bible Study/35–40 Minutes
☐ Going Further/25–30 Minutes*
*Optional

If you have only 50 minutes, move to the C-Group Warm-Up immediately. If you have 2½ hours, the Further Study can be incorporated into the regular meeting time. If not, you can assign this as homework for those interested in pursuing the subject further. For an older, or more mature group, you can condense the time required for the Starter Bible Study and spend more time on the Further Study.

Materials required:

☐ Student Books
☐ Pens
☐ Equipment for Crowd Breakers

Leadership: Note the 'Leaders' Checklist'.

22

IF YOU DO NOT HAVE TIME FOR THE FURTHER STUDY, review the material yourself as a short presentation which you will give at the end of the Starter Bible Study.

Meal: Ask a mum or dad to prepare an inexpensive but filling hot meal and ask everyone to bring the appropriate sum of money.

Crowd Breakers: Select one or two from the box and bring the extra supplies that are needed.

Review: If you assigned the Further Study as homework, take a moment and ask how it went.

 **WARM UP
C-Groups/8–10
Minutes**

Funny Faces

WELCOME the group.
DISTRIBUTE the books. ASK them to turn to Session 4.
READ the instructions for the Warm-Up—Funny Faces—and SHARE what kind of face you would draw in the first two circles.
GIVE them about 3 minutes in silence to draw their funny faces. Then, JOIN with their C-Groups and SHARE their drawings. (C-Group leader goes first.)

 **STARTER BIBLE
STUDY
C-Groups/35–40
Minutes**

Peter's Ups and Downs

EXPLAIN the directions for 'Peter's ups and downs.' SHOW them the graph and explain the 'feeling' scale from −5 (near to suicide) to +5 (natural high). EXPLAIN who Peter was. EXPLAIN that his name was changed from Simon to Cephas (meaning 'the rock') by Jesus.

GIVE an example of where you would put the 'dot' for the first episode (the first Bible passage). For instance, if you think he was moderately 'high,' you might put the dot on +2 in the A column. DON'T LABOUR the point, but make sure they understand the graphing idea before you proceed.

(Preparation, 3–5 Minutes) READ the first Bible episode (A) and pause for everyone IN SILENCE to put the dot in column A to indicate how Peter felt after that event.

Then, READ the next Bible episode and pause for everyone IN SILENCE to put the dot in column B, etc. . . . Continue until all 7 episodes have been read. CONNECT the dots to form a graph line.

(Discussion, 7–10 Minutes) REGATHER in C-Groups and SHARE your graph lines. DISCUSS these three questions:

☐ What does this tell about Peter?

☐ How does Peter's up-and-down life make you feel?

☐ Do you think he had more or less ups and downs than you have had?

(Preparation/Discussion, 15 Minutes) STOP the discussion for 2 or 3 minutes while everyone IN SILENCE completes the questions under 'My Own Story.' Then, REGATHER again for discussion.

(Leader's Note: This discussion will require more honesty on the part of the group members, but after four weeks together, they should be ready. APPEAL to the best in them without making it 'heavy'. This will be an excellent opportunity for you to feel the spiritual pulse of your group and the individuals in it. *During the week, you may want to follow up those in your Group, to help them in their particular struggles.)*

MOVE to the instructions in the Further Study and present the main points yourself if you do not have time for the Further Study in full.

CLOSE with a large fellowship circle. Ask if anyone would like to share a one-sentence prayer before you give the final prayer.

GOING FURTHER
All together/25–30 Minutes

My Ups and Downs

If you have time, work together on the Further study with everyone together. READ the question aloud and let anyone share the answer. ALLOW for discussion. Divide the time equally over the 6 questions.

If you do not have time, MAKE a presentation yourself covering the main points and discuss these points with the group:

☐ Jesus Christ loves us and walks with us through these ups and downs.

☐ Jesus has freed us from having to live the yo-yo existence we sometimes live.

☐ Romans 8:14–16 explains how a loving Father treats his children when they are going through hard times.

☐ Romans 8:28 explains how God can work things out for the good.

☐ Romans 8:37–39 explains that nothing can separate us from the love of God.

Optional Crowd Breakers

SUITCASE RELAY (*For two or more teams*)
Divide the group into equal teams—as many boys as girls in each. Give each team a suitcase. In each suitcase is a lady's dress and a man's suit—complete with shirt and tie. On the word GO, a *first* couple (boy and girl) from each team must run with their suitcase to the opposite end of the room, open the suitcase, and put on everything in the suitcase—the boy putting on the lady's dress and the girl putting on the man's suit. Then they carry their suitcase back to the starting line. Undress. Put the clothes back into the suitcase and hand the suitcase to the *next* couple. The first team to complete the relay wins.

THUMPER (*For C-Groups*)
This game is played exactly like rhythm (see Session 2). But instead of a number, each person creates a 'sign'—such as (a) hands on head, (b) scratching your ear, (c) moving like a baboon, etc. Everyone thinks up their own 'sign' and shows this 'sign' to their group.

Then, on the word GO, you begin the rhythm: (a) slap your knees once, (b) clap your hands once, etc. Then, instead of snapping your right fingers, the 'number 1' person (c) shows his/her 'sign' . . . and then (d) someone else's 'sign.'

Then, you repeat the rhythm: (a) slap your knees, (b) clap your hands . . . and (c) the person whose 'sign' was shown proceeds to repeat his/her 'sign' and (d) shows someone else's 'sign.'

In other words, instead of saying *your* number and then *someone else's* number, you show *your* 'sign' and then *someone else's* 'sign.' The object is to keep the rhythm.

To begin, everyone slaps their knees and claps their hands. Then, the C-Group leader will give his/her 'sign' and someone else's 'sign.'

THIRD DEGREE (*For two teams*)
The leader divides the group into two teams, one composed of FBI members, the other of spies. Each spy is given a card bearing one of the instructions listed below, each spy receiving a different instruction. The FBI members then take turns asking questions of specific spies, calling out the name of each spy before asking the question. The FBI members may ask as many questions of as many or as few spies as they decide, and may ask any questions they wish (except about the instructions the spies were given). Each spy must answer each question asked him, but always in the manner described on his card. Whenever a spy's instruction is guessed correctly by an FBI member, that spy is eliminated from the game. The questions continue until all the spies' instructions are guessed correctly. If a spy gives an answer without following his instructions, he is eliminated.

Scores are kept for individuals rather than for teams. The winning spy is the one who has the most questions asked him before his instructions are guessed correctly. The winning FBI member is the one who guesses correctly the most number of instructions. (An FBI member may make a guess at any time, whether it is his turn to ask a question or not.)

1. Lie during every answer.
2. Answer each question as though you were (name of leader).
3. Try to start an argument with each answer you give.
4. Always state the name of some colour in each answer.
5. Always use a number in your answers.
6. Be evasive—never actually answer a question.
7. Always answer a question with a question.
8. Always exaggerate your answers.
9. Always pretend to misunderstand the questions by your answers.
10. Always scratch during your answers.
11. Always insult the questioner.
12. Always begin each answer with a cough.
13. Always mention some kind of food during each answer.

LEADERS' CHECKLIST

BEFORE THE SESSION

☐ Student Books: Have enough for newcomers.

☐ Meal: Ask someone to prepare the hot meal.

☐ Crowd Breakers: Choose one or two and collect the special equipment necessary.

☐ Absentees: Ask the C-Group leaders to contact anyone from their group who was absent last week.

☐ Team Training: Get together for support and go over the Bible study.

DURING THE SESSION

☐ Welcome: Welcome newcomers. Give them a book and assign to a C-Group.

☐ Modelling: C-Group Leaders 'go first' on sharing the funny faces in the Warm-Up.

☐ Change of pace: Note the change of pace for both Bible studies. In the Starter Bible Study, everyone works alone as you read aloud the Bible episodes and each shares his or her graph with their C-Group. If you don't have time to do the Further study share the main points yourself.

AFTER THE SESSION

☐ Collect: Collect the Student Books.

☐ Reorder: Order more Student Books.

☐ Team: Get together and evaluate the session.

Session 5
Belonging

Objectives: To help group members discover their part in loving each other according to John 13; to affirm one another in their strengths; to evaluate areas where further growth is needed; to continue to build a learning, loving, sharing, caring community.

Setting: Room large enough for large-group games with a cosy corner for C-Groups when they settle down for sharing.

Time: From 50 minutes to 2½ hours
- [ ] Meal/40 Minutes*
- [ ] Crowd Breakers/30 Minutes*
- [ ] C-Group Warm-Up/10–12 Minutes
- [ ] Starter Bible Study/35–40 Minutes
- [ ] Going Further/25–30 Minutes*
*Optional

If you have only 50 minutes, move to the C-Group Warm-Up immediately. If you have 2½ hours, the Further study can be incorporated into the regular meeting time. If not, you can assign this as homework for those interested in pursuing the subject further. For an older, or more mature group, you can condense the time required for the Starter Bible Study and spend more time on the Further study as a group.

Materials required:
- [ ] Student Books
- [ ] Pens
- [ ] Equipment for Crowd Breakers

Leadership: Continue meeting with your Youth Worker Team and C-Group leaders to support one another and go over the lesson plan before the youth meeting. Also, study the 'Leaders' Checklist'.

Meal: Ask a mum or dad to prepare an inexpensive but filling hot meal and let everyone know how much money to bring.

Crowd Breakers: Choose one or two to open the meeting. Some are for the whole group and some are for the small C-Groups.

Review: If you assigned the Further study for homework, take a few moments and ask what your Group got out of it.

 **WARM UP**
C-Groups/10–12
Minutes

Strength Bombardment

WELCOME the troops.
DISTRIBUTE the Student Books.
ASK them to gather with their C-Group. TURN to Session 5—Strength Bombardment.

READ the instructions carefully. ASK them to think of the others in their C-Group and jot down their names next to the quality you see most in them. (Leader: pick someone and explain where you would put this person's name. Set the pace for warm, genuine affirmation.)

After 2 or 3 minutes in silence, ASK the C-Groups to move in close. ASK one person in each group to sit in silence while the others explain where they put his/her name and why. Repeat this procedure until everyone in the group has been covered.

**STARTER BIBLE
STUDY
C-Groups/35–40
Minutes**

The Mark of the Disciple

READ the short selection from John 13 aloud to the entire group.

(Preparation, 7–10 Minutes) ASK everyone to work on their own (solo) on the questions under 'Looking into the Story' and 'My Own Story.' (No partners this session, for a change.)

Leader: Take a moment and explain the setting of this passage—The Last Supper—on the night before Jesus was crucified. READ John 13:1–10, about foot-washing, to the group.

(Discussion, 25–30 Minutes)
REGATHER in C-Groups and DISCUSS. CONCENTRATE on questions 4 and 5 under 'Looking into the Story' and all six questions from 'My Own Story.' EMPHASISE the point that the command Jesus gave his disciples wasn't just to be lived out 2000 years ago. It is a commandment for us today.

Then begin to PROBE gently, discovering how group members feel about this commandment in the light of their C-Group. Question 4 in 'My Own Story' provides more time for affirmation, and 5 and 6 give insights into personal needs. HELP members brainstorm on questions 5 and 6 on how they could grow in these areas. Help each person develop a personal growth plan for the week. *Then CHECK with each member of your C-Group during the week to see how they're doing.*

(Note to Leader: After this session, you will have a fairly good understanding of how well the group is doing as a group—how well the learning, caring, sharing goals have been met. If things are good, great. If not, talk with other members of the Youth Worker Team about how the group can improve.)

CLOSE in prayer in C-Groups. Your group might be ready for conversational prayer. If it seems appropriate, ask the groups to hold hands as they pray.

**GOING FURTHER
C-Groups/25–30
Minutes**

Personal Inventory

If you have time, ASK group members to work on the Further study alone (solo). Then, REGATHER in C-Groups and DISCUSS the results.

If you do not have time, you may like to allow the students to take their books home and do the Further study as homework. If you do this, you will have to phone the students before the next session and remind them to bring their books back.

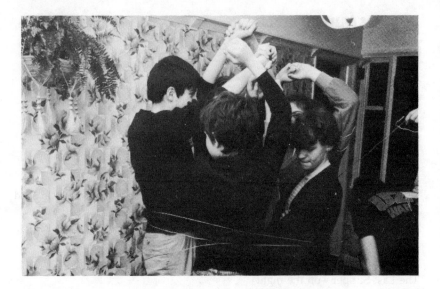

Optional Crowd Breakers

AMOEBA

Divide into teams and simply tie a rope around the team at their waists. To do this, have the team bunch up as close together as they can, and hold their hands up in the air while you tie the rope around them. After they are tied, they have to race to a goal and back. Unless they work together and co-operate as a team, they will go nowhere. This is a good game for camps and outdoor activities.

LINE PULL

Divide the group into two equal teams. The teams then face each other, by lining up on two sides of a line drawn on the floor. The object of the game is to pull the other team onto your side of the line. You cannot move behind your side of the line farther than three feet, and you must try to reach out and grab someone on the other side of the line without stepping over the line. Once you are over the line, you are automatically a member of that team and then you must try to help pull your former team over the line. At the end of the time period, the team with the largest number wins.

FILL THE MAT RELAY (For two or three teams)

Each team is given two mattresses on which to perform. A description is called out, then on the starting whistle each team begins to fulfill the description. First team to accurately fulfill this description is the winner. Suggested descriptions:

- ☐ 8 players standing shoulder to shoulder, facing in alternate directions

- ☐ 10 players in one huge pyramid (pyramid must remain standing)

- ☐ 4 people standing on their heads

- ☐ 10 contestants lying in a circle with feet together and holding hands like a huge wheel

- ☐ 8 people lying side by side with heads and feet in alternate directions

- ☐ 2 piles of 4 players each

- ☐ 6 players sitting on each other's laps

- ☐ entire team form a machine, with all parts moving in sequence.

CROWS AND CRANES

Divide players into two teams, one 'crows' and the other 'cranes'. Both teams line up across the play area facing each other about six feet apart. The leader stands midfield on the side and yells either 'crows' or 'cranes'. If leader calls 'crows,' the crows run and are chased by the cranes. If a crow is tagged by a crane before he/she reaches safety behind an appointed goal line, he/she becomes a crane. Both groups line up again quickly after each series, and the leader may repeat the same bird or call 'cranes.' If so, the crows chase the cranes. The team with the most players when time is called is the winner.

ROUNDUP

All the players are divided into two teams with the same number of boys and girls on each team. The girls of each team are the cowboys and the boys the cows. The cows must stay on their hands and knees throughout the game. The object of the game is this: the girls of each team try to get the cows of the opposing team into an area designated as the corral. The girls can drag, carry, etc., a cow to that area. Of course, the cows can resist but must stay on hands and knees. After a designated time interval, the team with the most cows in their corral wins.

LEADERS' CHECKLIST

BEFORE THE SESSION

☐ Student Books: Do you have enough.

☐ Meal: Do you have someone preparing this?

☐ Absentees: Ask the C-Group leaders to contact their members who were absent last week.

☐ Research: Read John 13 for the background to the Bible passage. Be prepared to give a short explanation of the Bible passage before the Starter Bible Study.

DURING THE SESSION

☐ Welcome: Welcome newcomers. Give them a book and assign them to a C-Group.

☐ Warm-Up Exercise: This exercise is potent but it must be demonstrated. Give an example by picking out one or two of the Group and telling them one or two of the good qualities you see in them.

☐ Change of pace: On the Starter Bible Study, note the change of pace— everyone works alone on the exercise instead of with a partner.

AFTER THE SESSION

☐ Collect: Collect the Student Books unless you are assigning the Further study as homework.

☐ Team: Get together with your Youth Worker Team. Evaluate the session and think about the future together.

☐ Celebration: Think about something special to close the course after session 7.

Session 6
Hanging In There

Objectives: To help group members examine their own spiritual commitment to Jesus Christ in the face of obstacles and hostility, to experience the forgiveness of God in situations where they've failed, and to continue to develop this kind of spiritual community in the C-Groups.

Setting: Plenty of room for the crowd breakers and a cosy corner for the C-Groups to meet in comfort and intimacy.

Time: From 50 minutes to 2½ hours
□ Meal/40 Minutes*
□ Crowd Breakers/30 Minutes*
□ C-Group Warm-Up/8–10 Minutes
□ Starter Bible Study/35–40 Minutes
□ Going Further/25–30 Minutes*
*Optional

If you have only 50 minutes, move to the C-Group Warm-Up immediately. If you have 2½ hours, the Further Study can be incorporated into the regular meeting time. If not, you can assign this as homework for those interested in pursuing the subject further. For an older, or more mature group, you can condense the time required for the Starter Bible Study and spend more time on the Further Study as a group.

Materials required:

□ Student Books
□ Pens
□ Equipment for Crowd Breakers

Leadership: Meet once a week (apart from the youth meeting) for your own support and planning. Study the 'Leaders' Checklist'.

Meal: If you're planning a meal, make sure you've contacted a mum or dad to bring the food and that you've told everyone how much money to bring.

Crowd Breakers: Choose one or two and assign the team members to collect any equipment you may need.

Review: If you assigned the Further study for homework, take a few minutes and ask what they got out of their study.

 **WARM-UP C-Groups/8–10 Minutes**

Four Facts/One Lie

WELCOME the group.
DISTRIBUTE the books. ASK everyone to turn to Session 6.
READ the instructions carefully and GIVE everyone 2 minutes in silence to jot down their answers, making ONE of the 5 answers a LIE.
  GET TOGETHER in C-Groups and ask the C-Group leader to go first—to share his/her 5 statements and have the Group guess which statement is a lie.

Then, repeat the procedure with the next person, etc., until all in the C-Group have read their 5 statements and the others have guessed which is the lie.

CONCENTRATE on the point that with God our failures can be turned into positive elements in our lives.

If you will not have time for the Further study, TEACH the group that they can experience God's forgiveness for failures in their lives. SHARE 1 John 1:9.

CLOSE in prayer. ASK any members of the group if they'd like to pray aloud.

STARTER BIBLE STUDY
C-Groups/35–40 Minutes

Peter Bails Out

SELECT someone in advance to read the text from Luke 22:54–62.

(Preparation, 8–10 Minutes) ASK the C-Groups to split into pairs and work together on the questions under 'Looking into the Story.' Then, continue on their own (solo) on 'My Own Story' questions. Questions 5 and 6 in 'My Own Story' take some special thought. You may want to HELP those who are struggling with those questions.

(Discussion, 20–25 Minutes) CALL the groups back together and DISCUSS. Look at all the questions—both the ones from 'Looking into the Story' and from 'My Own Story.'

HELP the group to get a feel for Peter's predicament. Help them to get into the shoes of this fisherman. Aim at a real understanding of Peter's failure and the fact that his denial did not ruin his relationship with Jesus.

With the first four questions of 'My Own Story', ENCOURAGE members of the group to brainstorm ways on how they might be stronger in the future. In Questions 5 and 7,

GOING FURTHER
C-Groups/25–30 Minutes

God's Forgiveness and Me

This is a *very important* study because every Christian needs to understand God's forgiving love and apply it throughout his/her lifetime. ASK the Group members to work in pairs on this material.

GIVE them most of the time to work together. CENTRE the discussion only on what they learned from working on the questions together. Don't focus on each question.

Optional Crowd Breakers

CRICKET TWIST (for two or three teams)
Teams line up in normal relay fashion. At a point some 20 or 30 feet away, a team captain or leader stands and holds a cricket bat. When the game begins, each player runs to his team leader, takes the cricket bat, holds it against his or her nose with the other end on the ground. Then the player must turn around as fast as possible ten times, while the leader counts the number of turns. Then the player hands the cricket bat back to the leader, runs back to the team, and tags the next player who does the same. Players become very dizzy and the results are hilarious.

EXPANDABLE FLOPSCOTCH
This is a grown-up version of the old child's game of hopscotch. Secure small-size carpet remnants from any carpet store. These are the hopscotch squares. The game is played as usual, except that the squares are spaced further and further apart as the game progresses until the players are jumping several feet between squares. It's good competition and is great for laughs.

CRAZY CREATIVE SCAVENGER HUNT
Here's a fun variation of the old scavenger hunt. Give each team a list of crazy names (such as the following sample list). Each team has to go out and collect items that they think best fit the names on the list. For example:

- □ A P B J
- □ Zipper zapping shoestring fuse
- □ Hollywood
- □ Tweed
- □ Snail Egg
- □ Chicken Lips
- □ Will be
- □ Pine Needle Bushing Brush
- □ Owl
- □ Piano Key Moustache Waxer
- □ Sludgegulper
- □ Portable Electric Door Knob Kneeler
- □ Thumb Twiddly Dummer
- □ Thingamabob
- □ An Inflatable Deflater
- □ Galvanized Ghoul Gooser

A panel of judges can determine the winners based on each team's explanation of how their 'items' fit the various descriptions on the list.

LEADERS' CHECKLIST

BEFORE THE SESSION

☐ Student Books: Make sure you have enough.

☐ Meal: Check with the parent who is preparing the meal.

☐ Absentees: Ask the C-Group leaders to contact their absentees.

☐ Crowd Breakers: Choose one or two and get the C-Group leaders to bring the equipment.

☐ Team Training: Get together with your C-Group leaders and go over the lesson before the youth meeting.

DURING THE SESSION

☐ Welcome: Welcome newcomers. Give them books and assign them to a C-Group.

☐ Warm-Up: Demonstrate the warm-up exercise yourself, letting your Group members guess which of the five facts about yourself is the lie.

☐ Starter Bible Study: Prepare your C-Group leaders to stress the 'forgiveness' aspect of God's love in the discussion.

☐ Prayer: Note the opportunity for Group members to lead in prayer. If this is strange in your tradition, talk a little about praying to God naturally.

AFTER THE SESSION

☐ Collect: Collect the Student Books

☐ Next week: Next week is the last session in this course. You may want to plan a special worship service or party at the close.

Session 7
Next Step

Objectives: To complete the course successfully; to *be* a loving, caring, sharing community for one another; to evaluate personally what has happened during the course and prepare for what still needs to take place; to determine the next step.

Setting: If you are planning a worship service or party to conclude this session, you may have to use a different room.

Time: From 50 minutes to 2½ hours
□ Meal/40 Minutes*
□ C-Group Warm-Up/8–10 Minutes
□ Starter Bible Study/25–30 Minutes
□ Summing Up/10–15 Minutes*
□ Worship Service or Party*
*Optional

If you have only 50 minutes, move to the C-Group Warm-Up immediately. If you have 2½ hours, the special Summing Up exercise can be incorporated into the regular meeting time.

Also, you may wish to conclude the course with a time of worship and sharing. Special instructions for these options are given on the next page.

Materials required:
□ Student Books
□ Pens
□ Refreshments for party, or materials for worship service.

Leadership: At the team meeting, discuss the options for concluding this course.

Meal: If you're planning a meal, make sure that you've contacted the parent preparing it, and remind the group members to bring their money.

Review: If you assigned the Further study last week for homework, take a few minutes and let the group share what they learned.

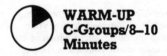

WARM-UP
C-Groups/8–10 Minutes

Advertising Slogans

WELCOME the group.
DISTRIBUTE the books. ASK them to turn to Session 7. READ the directions carefully. (Pause a moment and give an example.)

Then, ASK the C-Groups to get together and sit in silence until everyone has jotted down the names of the others in their C-Group next to the slogan that applies to each person.

Then, ASK the C-Group leader in each group to sit in silence while the rest of their C-Group explains the slogan they picked for him/her. Then, ask the next person to sit in silence . . . until everyone has been affirmed.

STARTER BIBLE STUDY
C-Groups/25–30 Minutes

The Go-For-It Bereans

SELECT someone in advance to read the Bible passage aloud to the entire group.

(Preparation, 6–10 Minutes)
ENCOURAGE the group to work in pairs on the questions under 'Looking into the Story' and 'My Own Story.'

(Discussion, 15–20 Minutes)
REGATHER in C-Groups and DISCUSS the questions. FOCUS on 'My Own Story' questions 5 and 6. DETERMINE what kind of help or resources they need to continue in their own study of the Bible, and help meet their needs.

CLOSE in prayer. If it seems appropriate, ask C-Group members to hold hands and ENCOURAGE anyone who wants to pray to do so.

SUMMING-UP EXERCISES
C-Groups/10–15 Minutes

Flashback 1

TURN back to the beginning of the Student Books. Read the instructions and ASK everyone to put the two symbols on the cricket pitch to indicate where they are now in these two relationships.

REGATHER with the C-Groups and explain where they placed the symbols.

Then if there is time, answer these three questions:

☐ If you had to compare your spiritual life right now to a cricket pitch, what is the 'throw'? (Such as: a tie score)

☐ What has the last innings (the last 6 weeks) been like? (Such as: a few errors, or a home run)

☐ What is your plan for the next innings?

Flashback 2

TURN to Session 1. PAUSE for a moment to decide which of the soils described in the Starter Study show how you are receiving the 'seed' of God's Word now. Then, SHARE with your C-Group what you have chosen.

Instant Replay

TURN to the Summing Up exercise for Session 7. PAUSE for a moment to let each student complete the 5 questions. Then REGATHER in C-Groups and SHARE one question at a time.

CLOSING
All Together/Open-ended

To celebrate your experience during this course, here are two options:

Quaker Service: This is sometimes called a testimonial meeting.

Move to a quiet, meditative place, such as a church building . . . or turn out the lights and light a fire . . . or candles. Begin the service by explaining a little about the Quaker tradition and the importance of being in silence . . . letting God speak to us before we speak to him or to others.

To introduce the period of silence, lead the group in singing together a meditative hymn or chorus to focus the attention. Then wait in silence until someone breaks the silence with their sharing.

Suggest that the sharing be limited to the 'next steps' in their spiritual journey . . . and where they need the support of the community in their venture.

Set the pace with your own example. Make it personal, very specific . . . and honest.

Commissioning Service. Change the atmosphere in the room or move to another place. This service is best carried out in small clusters—with people that know each other.

Give each person in the group a chance to explain the 'next step' in their life . . . or what 'God is asking me to do.' Then have this person kneel or sit in the centre of the group while the others in the group commission this person to the task they have explained, one person praying for the whole group while everyone 'lays their hands' on the head or shoulders.

Then the next person explains where they need to move out . . . and kneels in the group to be commissioned and prayed for, until everyone has been commissioned.

KNOWING ME:

On My Identity

1 **MY SPECIALNESS**
   Exodus 3 and 4

2 **MY INTERESTS**
   Luke 10:38–42

3 **MY ABILITIES**
   Matthew 25:14–30

4 **MY PROBLEMS**
   Genesis 37–45

5 **MY VALUES**
   Luke 18:18–25

6 **MY FAITH**
   John 20:24–31

7 **MY TOMORROW**
   Matthew 10:35–38

'I can do everything through him who gives me strength.'

Philippians 4:13, NIV

CONTENTS

WARM-UP

to build trust and
confidence in the
C-Groups before
the Bible study

STARTER BIBLE STUDY

to share 'my own
story' in the
C-Groups through
a Bible story

GOING FURTHER

to go deeper into the
Bible

---

1 MY SPECIALNESS

Back to Back
Sit back to back with one
other and try to guess a
few things about your
partner. 'My partner is
someone who would . . .
shout at a referee . . . only
buy Levi jeans . . .' etc.
Then turn around and
compare.

The Calling of Moses
Moses, the reluctant
leader, becomes the 'story'
in which you talk about
your own specialness. Each
study group starts its time
together.

About Me . . . and My Specialness
Why am I so special? How
do I know God thinks I'm
special? Here's a chance to
put the same value on
yourself that God puts on
you. Write a note to God
about this.

---

2 MY INTERESTS

My Favourite Things
How do you spend your
time? Make a list of the
things most teenagers like
to do, in the order of
popularity. Would you
rather 'go shopping . . .
listen to music . . . talk on
the phone . . . work on
your car,' etc.?

Martha and Mary
You try to help Martha,
who has been surprised by
Jesus. How does her 'story'
compare with what
interests you, bugs you,
pushes your panic button?
See your 'story' through
Martha's 'story.'

About Me . . . and My Interests
Draw a pie-chart of your
time—how you spend your
free time. Compare your
time priorities with the
Bible. Check your weekly
expense account to see
how you spend your
money. Determine how to
choose between 'better'
and 'best.'

---

3 MY ABILITIES

Talent Scout Report
If you were your own
talent scout, how would
you rate your strengths: (a)
mental, (b) emotional, and
(c) spiritual? Get together
with your group and see if
they see things you
missed.

The Hidden Talent
Take a look at the three
servants who use their
talents in various ways.
Ask these questions: How
have I used my talents?
How have I hidden them?
Compare the 'story' in the
Bible to your 'story.'

About Me . . . and My Abilities
Why get excited about
discovering 'my gift' and
using it? See what the Bible
has to say about gifts,
talents, and abilities and
complete a fill-in prayer
about the talents God has
given to you.

On My Identity

4 MY PROBLEMS

Problem Survey
List the problems teenagers face in your community in the order of seriousness—1 to 14. Then get together with someone else and try to agree on the top 5 before sharing with your own Group.

Joseph's Story
Joseph, the man with many problems, overcomes. Use his 'story' to examine your own troubles and learn the secret to being an overcomer too.

About Me ... and My Problems
Take a look at some of the many promises in the Bible in the light of your own problems. Pray with your partner about your problems.

5 MY VALUES

Values Auction
You've been given £1000 to bid on fifteen items. How will you spend your money? Here's a chance for you to decide on what's important in your life right now.

The Rich Young Ruler
Get into the mind of a rich man with misplaced values. Discover your own values and decide what you need to do to keep wrong values from becoming number 1.

About Me ... and My Values
Learn what it means to value God as number 1 in your life. . . . Think how you can let God transform the values area of your life. Spend time with your partner in prayer.

6 MY FAITH

Trust Walk
Go on a 'walk by faith', allowing your partner to lead you in 'new areas'—blindfolded. Then reverse the roles. Sit down and talk about your feelings.

Thomas, the Honest Doubter
Live through the agony of the death of Christ with Thomas and see if you can understand his doubts about the resurrection. Where are the question marks in your faith?

About Me ... and My Faith
Why is faith so important? What does it mean? Look at some of the great people of faith in the Bible for a model, and compare their example to your own life.

7 MY TOMORROW

Summing Up
How have you changed during this course? Where do you need to grow? What would you like to do next? Look into the future and dream a little.

Workers and Harvest
Are you part of the harvest or part of the work force? God loves you. What do you want to do about it? Here's a chance for you to evaluate what you are doing with your life.

Job Centre
Your local job centre is advertising a few jobs and you are asked to recommend people from your Group. Who would you recommend for the job of athletics coach . . . drama producer . . . caretaker?

Session 1
My Specialness

Objectives: To get better acquainted with one another, to form C-Groups for the first time, to help *all* members of the group realise that they are special, that God created them, that God knows them, and that God loves them. And that they are loved by you too.

Setting: Casual, informal atmosphere—movable chairs or a rug on the floor—where the C-Groups can gather and where the crowd breakers can be played.

Time: From 50 minutes to 2½ hours
- □ Meal/40 Minutes*
- □ Crowd Breakers/30 Minutes*
- □ C-Group Warm-Up/10 Minutes
- □ Starter Bible Study/40 Minutes
- □ Going Further/30 Minutes*

*Optional

If you have only 50 minutes, move to the C-Group Warm-Up immediately. If you have 2½ hours, the Further study can be incorporated into the regular meeting time. If not, you can assign this as homework for those interested in pursuing the subject further. For an older, or more mature group, you can condense the time required for the Starter Bible Study and spend more time on the Further study.

Materials required:
- □ Student Books
- □ Pens
- □ Special equipment for Crowd Breakers

Leadership: Study the 'Leaders' Checklist'.

Meal: Make sure you've contacted a mum or dad to prepare the meal. Charge the young people whatever is appropriate to cover the cost of the meal, and give the total to the parents providing it. Invest in some paper napkins, plates and cups, to reduce washing-up to a minimum.

Crowd Breakers: If you have time, start off the meeting with group-building games or mixers, selected from the crowd breakers. The magazine collage will take 30 minutes to make and share in pairs. The others are more for mixing up the group and having fun.

INTRODUCTION
All Together/3 Minutes

Welcome

Welcome the group and introduce them to this session. Say something like: 'I want to welcome every one of you here. For the next 7 weeks, we're going to focus on one subject—our identity—through a course called *Knowing Me*. (Hand out the student Books, and pens, to each student.) Open your booklet to inside the front cover and we'll review some of the subjects we'll be looking at over the next few weeks.'

Go through the overview, quickly touching on the topics—My Specialness, My Interests, etc.— without going into much detail. After you've finished the overview continue by saying something like. . . .

'Each week we'll begin the study session with a warm-up exercise that relates to the subject of the week and that helps us get to know each other better. Then, we will take time to share the exercise in a small group—called a C-Group. Each C-Group is composed of 4–6 students (or whatever your number is for your group) and one leader. The C-Groups for this course will be: (read off the names of the people in each C-Group—together with the person from the Youth Worker Team who will be their leader. Make sure you have places for those teenagers whom you didn't anticipate in advance).'

ASK them to join their C-Groups at different parts of the room. As soon as they've grouped, MOVE to the Warm-Up.

WARM-UP
C-Groups/10 Minutes

Back to Back

Step 1: ASK each person to choose a partner from their C-Groups, and TURN to Session 1 in their books. Then READ the directions to them: 'Sit back to back with your partner and guess what answer your partner would give to each of these questions. As soon as you've both finished, compare your answers.

Give yourself 10 points for every correct guess about your partner. When you have scored your results, MOVE on to the 2 questions at the bottom and DISCUSS these.'

Leader: After about 5 minutes ask the partners to regather with their C-Group and introduce their partner to the group by telling something 'special' they found out about their partner.

Step 2: ASK them to turn to the diagram of the football ground. SAY something like: 'To begin this course, I'd like all of us to think about where we are right now with God. This little diagram will help us. Follow me while I read.'

READ the directions in the Student Book aloud and give them 1 minute to place their 'x' on the diagram. Then, ASK them to return to their partner and share. *(Take a moment and explain where you would put your 'x'. Set an example of openness and honesty.)*

STARTER BIBLE STUDY
C-Groups/40 Minutes

The Calling of Moses

MOVE to the Starter Bible Study for Session 1. SAY something like: 'Now let's begin our study on why we're so special. Turn to the Starter Bible Study.'

In advance, SELECT a student who is a good reader and who would be happy to read the Bible passage. SAY something like: 'I asked Mike several days ago to read this for us. Please follow along as he reads.'

(Open discussion, 7 Minutes) After the passage has been read, TAKE a few minutes to ASK and REFLECT on these questions. *(Try to get the groups' answers before sharing yours.)*

- *What do you know about Moses?* (He grew up in Egypt; he killed a man and ran away from that country for fear of being caught and punished for his action; he had spent 40 years in the wilderness tending sheep when this story takes place.)

- *What do you know about Pharaoh?* (Leader of Egypt, one of the most powerful nations at that time.)

- *What do you know about the Israelites?* (Over a million Israelites were employed as slave labour. God wanted to free them.)

ALLOW about 7 minutes for these 3 questions.

(Preparation, 10 Minutes) With that background, ASK them to work with a partner on the 4 questions in 'Looking into the Story.' Then, work solo on the questions under 'My Own Story.' At the end of 5 or 10 minutes, ASK them to rejoin their groups.

(Discussion, 20 Minutes) In C-Groups, DISCUSS the answers to all questions. Especially focus on 'My Own Story,' questions 3, 4, 5 and 7. The point: to help every person really know that he/she is a special person created and loved by God. Help the reluctant students to answer number 7 and to be affirmed by other members of the group that yes, those are good qualities.

As a leader of the C-Group, close in prayer, thanking God for the special qualities of each member of the group.

GOING FURTHER
C-Groups/30 Minutes

About Me . . . and My Specialness

If you have time, first have everyone work solo on questions 1–5. Then REGATHER in C-Groups and discuss each question. Especially focus on question 4 (He likes everyone best—because we are all special) and question 5.

Then, SOLO, have group members write and pray the prayer to God.

Optional Crowd Breakers

If you have the time, the space, and the energy, starting off the youth meeting with one or two of these crowd breakers would be an excellent way to prepare the group for this session. Note the extra materials that are needed for each crowd breaker.

MAGAZINE COLLAGE
Leaf through a colour magazine or daily newspaper and tear out some pictures, words, slogans, adverts, etc., that reveal who you are: (1) your interests, (2) your self-image—how you see yourself, (3) your special abilities, and (4) your outlook on life. After 10 minutes, collect your 'tear-outs' and paste them on a sheet of newsprint or poster paper. Then, get together with one or two others and explain your 'self-portrait'. *Materials required:* □ Pictorial magazine or newspaper for everyone □ newsprint sheet or poster paper for everyone □ glue □ SAMPLE collage to demonstrate how it is done.

BIRTHDAY TURNOVER

Have everyone sit in a circle with the same number of chairs as there are people. 'It' stands in the centre without a chair. He calls out any number of months of the year. After the last month is called, everyone who has a birthday during one of those months gets up and tries to take another seat. 'It' also tries to find a vacant seat. Whoever is left without a seat becomes 'it.'

CLUMPS

This game may be used for as many as 1000. Everyone crowds to the centre with arms at sides. They are instructed to keep moving, but crowd toward the centre. They must keep their arms at their sides. The leader blows a whistle or foghorn to stop all movement, and immediately yells out a number. If the number is 4, for instance, everyone must get into groups of 4, lock arms, and sit down. Leaders then eliminate all those not in groups of 4. This process is repeated, with different numbers each time, until all have been eliminated.

SHUFFLE

Arrange chairs in a circle so each person has a chair. There should be two extra chairs in the circle. Each person sits in a chair except for two people in the middle who try to sit in the two vacant chairs. The persons sitting on the chairs keep moving around from chair to chair to prevent the two in the middle from sitting down. If one or both of the two in the middle manage to sit in a chair, the person on their right replaces them in the middle of the circle and then tries to sit in an empty chair.

LEADERS' CHECKLIST

BEFORE THE SESSION

☐ Student Books and pens: Make sure you have enough for everyone.

☐ C-Group Leaders: Make sure you have a leader for every 4 to 7 teenagers.

☐ Crowd Breakers: Pick one or two to start the meeting. Get the materials.

☐ Training: Go over the Bible study with your C-Group leaders.

☐ Research: Read about Moses in the first few chapters of Exodus.

DURING THE SESSION

☐ C-Groups: The objective of this session is to establish C-Groups. Divide the members into C-Groups and put one leader from the Youth Worker Team with each Group.

☐ Partners: The C-Group Warm-Up starts off in pairs—sitting back to back. If there is an odd number, the Group leader drops out.

☐ Model: Before each sharing experience, you *go first*. Set an example of sharing by your own openness and honesty.

AFTER THE SESSION

☐ Collect: Collect the Student Books unless you are assigning the 'Going Further' study as homework.

☐ C-Group Leaders: Get together and evaluate the session. Ask the Leaders to visit or phone the members of their group, this week.

☐ Order: Order more Student Books for newcomers.

☐ Special Event: Plan something special for the young people about half-way through the course. The YWT should organise the special event.

Session 2
My Interests

Objectives: To get better acquainted in C-Groups, to discover some of each other's interests, to realise that some interests are more lasting than others, to continue to encourage the development of a caring, loving community of people.

Setting: Casual, informal atmosphere—where the entire group can gather and where the crowd breakers can be played.

Time: From 50 minutes to 2½ hours
- ☐ Meal/40 Minutes*
- ☐ Crowd Breakers/30 Minutes*
- ☐ C-Group Warm-Up/12–15 Minutes
- ☐ Starter Bible Study/35–40 Minutes
- ☐ Going Further/25–30 Minutes*

*Optional

If you have only 50 minutes, move to the C-Group Warm-Up immediately. If you have 2½ hours, the Further study can be incorporated into the regular meeting time. If not, you can assign this as homework for those interested in pursuing the subject further. For an older, or more mature group, you can condense the time required for the Starter Bible Study and spend more time on the Further study.

Materials required:
- ☐ Student Books
- ☐ Pens
- ☐ Special equipment for Crowd Breakers

Leadership: Study the 'Leaders' Checklist'.

Meal: If you are planning a meal, make sure you've contacted a mum or dad for the food and have told the group members how much money they need to bring.

Crowd Breaker: Select one or two of the crowd breakers to start off the meeting if you have time. Some are for the group all together and some are for C-Groups together.

WARM UP
C-Groups/12–15 Minutes

My Favourite Things
WELCOME the group. ASK them to join their C-Groups. Ask each Group leader to DISTRIBUTE the pens and Student Books.
   Then READ the directions for 'My Favourite Things.' ASK them to work solo (in private) on the grading and to share their list with a partner from their Group. Then each Group should RE-GATHER and DISCUSS these three questions:

- ☐ Are any of these interests wrong in themselves?

- ☐ When might it be good to give time to these interests?

- ☐ When might it be bad to give time to these interests?

44

(The Point: Most of these interests are fine, fun, and helpful to becoming a well-rounded person. But sometimes other things are more important and have priority. You need to study. Your parents need you to help, etc. *Don't spend too much time commenting on these questions. The issues become more clear after the Starter Bible Study*).

Hopefully, members of the group will emerge with the feelings: it's important to have interests; I know what some of mine are; but it's even more important to realise that some interests have long-term worth and are more important than others.

CLOSE in prayer, thanking God for the interests he has given us.

STARTER BIBLE STUDY
C-Groups/35–40 Minutes

Martha and Mary

As a total group, have someone you've selected in advance READ the Bible passage from Luke 10:38–42. ASK the group what they know about Mary and Martha. (They were good friends of Jesus; their brother's name was Lazarus—a man Jesus raised from the dead.)

(Preparation, 10–12 Minutes) ASK each C-Group to split up into pairs and work on the questions in 'Looking into the Story.' Then work solo on the questions under 'My Own Story'. Plan on 10–12 minutes for this section but keep an eye on members of your C-Group and be ready to move to the discussion when everyone is finished.

(Discussion, 20 Minutes) Still in C-Groups, DISCUSS the questions under 'Looking into the Story'. Especially focus on question 6—to summarise the point of Jesus' comment to Martha. After 5 or 10 minutes move on to the 'My Own Story' section.

In 'My Own Story' section, CONCENTRATE on questions 2 to 6. Question 6 is especially important in helping each person summarise what they learned.

GOING FURTHER
C-Groups/25–30 Minutes

About Me . . . and My Interests

If you have enough time, ASK everyone to work on the pie chart and the questions individually and then discuss them. (With very little effort, the discussion could last 30 minutes itself.) But if time is limited, ask each person to take the Further study home and work on it there. *(Note: If they take their Student Books home, you'll probably have to contact them the day before the next meeting to remind them to bring their books back.)* Then, either schedule time at the next meeting for some reflection on the Further study and/or contact each person in your C-Group during the week and ask them what they learned from doing the Further study.

45

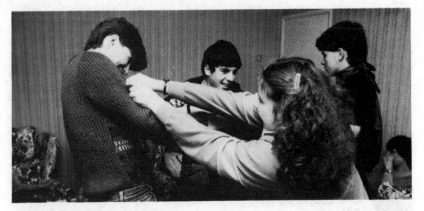

Optional Crowd Breakers

BLIND VOLLEYBALL
Divide the players into two equal
groups. The two teams then get on
different sides of a volleyball court and
sit down on the floor in a row. The 'net'
should be a solid divider that obstructs
the view of the other team, such as
blankets hung over a regular volleyball
net or rope. The divider should also be
low enough that players cannot see
under it. Then play volleyball. Use a
big, light plastic ball instead of a
volleyball. Regular volleyball rules and
boundaries apply. A player may not
stand up to hit the ball. The added
dimension of the solid net adds a real
surprise element to the game when the
ball comes flying over the net.

MOTORBOAT
Make believe your C-Group is a motor.
See how much speed you can achieve.
At the word GO, the first person turns
his head to the right, saying the sound
for the specified motor; then the next
person turns his head to the right,
repeating the sound; and so on round
the circle. The first group to finish the
number of laps should clap.

☐ Round One: *Go-carts* . . . for five laps
. . . and the sound is 'putt.'

☐ Round Two: Motorcycles . . . for
seven laps . . . and the sound is
'rrrrrrr. . . .'

☐ Round Three: Racing cars at Brands
Hatch . . . for twenty laps . . . and
the sound is 'zoooooommmmmmm.'

SNATCH
This is a good game for holiday or
outdoor events, and is best used with
younger teenagers. The group is divided
into two teams each lined up behind its
goal line 20–30 feet apart. A towel tied
in the middle is placed at a point
halfway between goal lines. Each player
is given a number. The two teams are
numbered from opposite ends of the
line.

The leader calls out a number. The
player on each team having that number
runs to the centre and tries to snatch
the towel and return to his goal without
being touched by the other person. The
more skilled player will run into the
centre and hover over the towel until
such a time when he can snatch it and
run when his opponent is off guard.
Each successful return gains one point
for the team. After each successful tag
or score, the towel is returned to the
centre and another number is called.
Play for a designated number of points.
The leader should call numbers in a
manner designed to create suspense. All
numbers should be included, but it is
well to repeat a number now and then
to keep all players alert. Also, maintain
interest by calling two or more numbers
simultaneously, thereby involving four
or more players.

CARRIER BAG RELAY (*For two or more teams*)

Divide into teams with 10 people on each team. Have a carrier bag for each team with the following items in each:

☐ jar of baby food

☐ spring onion

☐ Can of coke

☐ Raw carrot

☐ Piece of cream cheese (wrapped in waxed paper)

☐ Mars bar

☐ Peanut-butter sandwich

☐ An orange

☐ An apple

☐ A banana

On signal, the first member of each team runs to his bag and must eat the first item he pulls out. Organisers should make sure items are satisfactorily finished before the person goes back and touches the next member of the team. First team to finish its bag wins.

SAFETY PINS

Give everyone in the group six safety pins. On GO each player tries to pin his safety pin on the other players' clothing. When you have put your six safety pins on other people, try to place any safety pin anyone has placed on you on someone else. At the end of the time limit (3 minutes), the person with the fewest safety pins is the winner.

LEADERS' CHECKLIST

BEFORE THE SESSION

☐ Student Books: Do you have enough?

☐ C-Groups: Ask each Group leader to contact the members of their Group.

☐ Meal: Contact person in charge of the meal.

☐ Crowd Breakers: Choose your crowd breakers and collect the material you need.

☐ Team: Go over the Bible study with your Group leaders.

DURING THE SESSION

☐ Welcome: Welcome any newcomers. Give out the Student Books. Write names on page 1.

☐ C-Groups: Get together in your Groups. Assign any newcomers to a C-Group.

☐ Partners: Inside of each C-Group, work in pairs on the exercise before getting together for sharing as a Group.

☐ Model: Before any sharing experience, you go first. Set an example of sharing by your own honest sharing.

AFTER THE SESSION

☐ Evaluation: Get together with your Youth Worker Team and evaluate the session.

☐ Student Books: Collect the Student Books unless you are assigning the Further study as homework.

☐ Books: Order more Student Books for newcomers.

☐ Social: Continue with plans for a special event for the whole group.

Session 3
My Abilities

Objectives: To continue building close relationships in your youth group and C-Groups, to understand the importance of using the talents that you have; to reflect on how well each person is using their talents.

Setting: Casual, informal atmosphere—movable chairs and room enough for crowd breakers.

Time: From 50 Minutes to 2½ hours

- ☐ Meal/40 Minutes*
- ☐ Crowd Breakers/30 Minutes*
- ☐ C-Group Warm-Up/12–15 Minutes
- ☐ Starter Bible Study/35–40 Minutes
- ☐ Going Further/25–30 Minutes*
*Optional

If you have only 50 minutes, move to the C-Group Warm-Up immediately. If you have 2½ hours, the Further study can be incorporated into the regular meeting time. If not, you can assign this as homework for those interested in pursuing the subject further. For an older, or more mature group, you can condense the time required for the Starter Bible Study and spend more time on the Further study.

Materials required:

- ☐ Student Books
- ☐ Pens
- ☐ Special Equipment for Crowd Breakers

Leadership: Review the 'Leaders' Checklist'.

48

Meal: If you are planning on a meal, make sure you've contacted a mum or dad for the food and that you've told the young people how much money to bring to cover the cost.

Crowd Breakers: Select one or two. Some are for the group all together and some are for the small C-Groups.

Review: If you assigned the Further study as homework in Session 2, you may want to talk about it before you move to the C-Group Warm-Up for this session. Assess your time and reschedule accordingly if you wish to add a discussion of the Further study of the last session.

WARM-UP
C-Groups/12–15 Minutes

Talent Scout Report

WELCOME everyone. ASK them to join their C-Groups and then pick a partner from their C-Group with whom they will work during this session.

DISTRIBUTE Student Books and pens. ASK newcomers to put their name on Page 1.

DIRECT everyone to Session 3. DESCRIBE the 'Talent Scout Report'. Each person is to tick two or three best points in each category. After they have done that, they will meet with a partner and discuss what they ticked. The partner can say whether he/she agrees with him/her. They can then complete the last part of the exercise where they list one trait in each area that they would like to improve. (Note: This Warm-Up is not as light as some of the others. So you will have to encourage everyone to approach it with some seriousness and not to be falsely modest. You may have to give definitions of some of the traits.)

Before they start sharing, take a moment and MODEL what you ticked in the 'Talent Scout Report' on yourself. Set an example of candour and healthy self-appreciation.

When the twosomes have finished, REGATHER in C-Groups to share your findings. Each Group leader should ASK, 'What would you like to share from your Talent Scout Report?' ENCOURAGE each person to share 3 things—what they ticked in a particular area, what they want to work on, and how they could improve.

(Discussion, 20 Minutes) Whenever all the members of a C-Group have completed their questions, that C-Group can regather for discussion.

In 'Looking into the Story', CONCENTRATE on questions 2, 4, and 5.

In 'My Own Story' spend most of your time again on questions 2, 4, and 5.

Hopefully, members of your C-Group will emerge with the feeling that they are talented and that they all have a responsibility to use their talents. Through question 5, help them develop a plan for using their talents more effectively.

CLOSE in prayer with members of each C-Group praying for the person on their right, remembering especially any need or desire this person shared.

STARTER BIBLE STUDY
C-Groups/35–40 Minutes

The Hidden Talent

SELECT someone in advance to read Matthew 25:14–30 (or read the passage yourself since it is so long) and ask them to read it now to the total group.

(Preparation, 10 Minutes) INSTRUCT everyone to go back to their partner in the Warm-Up and work together on the five questions in 'Looking into the Story.' Then work solo (in private) on the questions in 'My Own Story'.

GOING FURTHER
C-Groups/25–30 Minutes

About Me . . . and My Talents

If you have time, get together again with your partner and work on the questions in the Further study.

Then, REGATHER with your Group and discuss your responses to the Bible passage. Use the thoughts you have jotted down in the Personal Application when you pray at the close.

Optional Crowd Breakers

NOSE TO NOSE/BACK TO BACK

Have everyone stand in the centre of the room. Blow a whistle and call out either: *Nose to nose* . . . or *Back to back*. Everyone quickly finds a partner and stands with their partner accordingly.

Blow the whistle again and call out the instructions. Everyone must find a new partner and assume the position you called out. For greater excitement, speed up or slow down the cadence . . . and repeat the same instructions two or three times in a row.

BIRDIE ON THE PERCH

Split into 2 groups. One group forms a circle facing out. The other group forms a circle around the first circle. Pair off— one person from the INNER circle with one person from the OUTER circle— making partners. At the whistle, the INNER and OUTER circles move in opposite directions.

When the whistle blows a second time, the people in the OUTER circle kneel *where they are* on one knee . . . and their partner from the INNER circle runs from wherever they are and 'perches' on their partner's knee. THE LAST 'couple' to perch is OUT.

The second round begins with the whistle. Circles move in opposite directions. When the whistle blows, the OUTER circle kneels *where they are* and their partners in the INNER circle run and perch on their knees. The last couple to perch is OUT. Repeat this procedure until a winning couple is determined.

MURDER

This is a great indoor game. Place a number of slips of paper in a hat. There should be the same number of slips of paper as there are players. One of these slips of paper has the word 'detective' written on it, and another has the word 'murderer' on it. The rest of them are blank. Everyone draws a slip of paper from the hat. Whoever drew the word 'detective' announces himself, and it is his job to try to locate the murderer, who remains silent.

The detective leaves the room, and the room is darkened. All the players mill about the room and the 'murderer' silently slips up behind someone and very quietly whispers, 'You're dead,' in his ear. The victim counts to three, screams, and falls to the floor. The lights are turned on and the detective re-enters the room. He may then question the players for one minute or so and tries to guess the identity of the murderer. If he is correct, the murderer becomes the detective, and a new murderer is selected (by passing out the slips again). During the questioning, only the murderer may lie. All others must tell the truth.

BALLOON STOMP

Everyone receives a balloon and a piece of string. Each person blows up the balloon *completely* and ties it to his ankle with the string. (If the balloon is not full of air it won't pop.) Working individually or as a C-Group team, try to stomp on the other balloons without getting your balloon stomped on. The last person or C-Group with a balloon wins.

ONE FROG

Work together by C-Groups on this mathematical riddle about ten frogs in a pond. Starting with *one* frog, go around your Group and have each person add to the riddle:

- First person: *'One frog'*
- Second person: *'Two eyes'*
- Third person: *'Four legs'*
- Fourth person: *'In the pond'*
- Fifth person: *'Kerplunk'*
- Sixth person: *'Kerplunk'*

Then, you move to *two* frogs and double everything—just like two frogs:

- Next person: *'Two frogs'*
- Next person: *'Four eyes'*
- Next person: *'Eight legs'*
- Next person: *'In the pond'*
- Next person: *'In the pond'* (you need two 'in the ponds' for two frogs)
- Next person: *'Kerplunk'*
- Next person: *'Kerplunk'*
- Next person: *'Kerplunk'*
- Next person: *'Kerplunk'*

The object of the game is to count up to ten frogs without making a mistake. IF ANYONE IN YOUR GROUP MAKES A MISTAKE, YOU MUST GO BACK TO 'ONE FROG' AND START ALL OVER AGAIN.

The first C-Group that gets to *ten frogs* stands up and cheers.

(Leader: Conduct a practice—with everyone repeating after you the parts of ONE frog— so that everyone understands the riddle. Then remind them that they must go back to ONE frog if anyone in their group makes a mistake).

LEADERS' CHECKLIST

BEFORE THE SESSION

- Student Books: Do you have enough? If the Group members took their books home, phone and remind them to bring their books.
- Meal: Is someone preparing the food?
- Crowd Breakers: Check to see if you have the extra material for the crowd breakers. Practise the instructions on 'One Frog'.
- Absentees: Ask the C-Group Leaders to contact any member of their Group who was absent last time.
- Research: Look up the word 'talents' in a Bible Dictionary.

DURING THE SESSION

- Welcome: Welcome newcomers. Give them a book. Write their names on page 1.
- C-Groups: When you get together in C-Groups, assign newcomers to a C-Group.
- Partners: Inside your C-Groups, all the exercises are first worked on in pairs. If there is an odd number, make groups of three.
- Model: Go first in the sharing, with an example of real honesty and openness.

AFTER THE SESSION

- Evaluation: Get together with your Youth Worker Team and evaluate the session.
- Student Books: Collect the Student Books unless you are assigning the Further study as homework.
- Order: Order more Student Books for newcomers.
- Retreat: Think about an overnight retreat to conclude the course.

Session 4
My Problems

Objectives: To realise that everyone has problems; to understand that God wants to help everyone with their problems; to know that by trusting God and trying to see things from his perspective, problems can be overcome; to continue to build a loving, caring community in the youth group.

Setting: Casual—with plenty of room for the crowd breakers and a cosy corner for settling down in C-Groups.

Time: From 50 minutes to 2½ hours

☐ Meal/40 Minutes*

☐ Crowd Breakers/30 Minutes*

☐ C-Group Warm-Up/12–15 Minutes

☐ Starter Bible Study/35–40 Minutes

☐ Going Further/25–30 Minutes*

*Optional

If you have only 50 minutes, move to the C-Group Warm-Up immediately. If you have 2½ hours, the Further study can be incorporated into the regular meeting time. If not, you can assign this as homework for those interested in pursuing the subject further. For an older, or more mature group, you can condense the time required for the Starter Bible Study and spend more time on the Further study.

Materials required:

☐ Student Books

☐ Pens

☐ Special Equipment for Crowd Breakers

Leadership: Read the 'Leaders' Checklist'.

Meal: If you are planning a meal, make sure you've contacted a mum or dad to bring the food and told the group members how much money to bring to cover the cost.

Crowd Breakers: Select one or more. There are some for the entire group and some for the C-Groups.

Review: If you assigned the Further Study as homework last week, you may want to take a moment and ask how the study went.

 WARM-UP C-Groups/12–15 Minutes

Problem Survey
WELCOME the troops. ASK them to join their C-Groups and to pair off within their Group for the Warm-Up exercise. (ENCOURAGE them not to choose the same partner each session).

DISTRIBUTE the Student Books and pens. Then DIRECT everyone to Session 4. ASK each person to work on the 'Problem Survey' alone. When everyone has finished listing the problems, GET TOGETHER with one other; compare lists. DEVELOP a new list. (Allow about 7 minutes for this.)

Now, JOIN with your other C-Group members and DISCUSS the

lists. Group leaders should ask: 'What did you select as numbers 1, 7, and 14? Why did you select those problems for those spots?' (Asking them to tell *only* numbers 1, 7, and 14, gives the Group a quick summary of what most people feel are the most important, least important, and 'medium-important' problems teenagers face.)

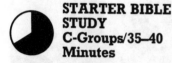

STARTER BIBLE STUDY
C-Groups/35–40 Minutes

Joseph's Story

ASK the students, as a total group, what they know about Joseph. Then GIVE a quick summary of Joseph's life. (As background, you will need to read Genesis 37 to 50.) A helpful outline might be: (1) From the pit, (2) to the pot (Potiphar), (3) to the prison, (4) to the palace. Don't go into too much detail; simply give them basic background information. Then ask a student you've selected in advance to READ the summary of Joseph's life. (Plan on about 5 minutes for the introduction and the reading.)

(Preparation, 10 Minutes) With their C-Group partners from the previous exercise, ASK them to work on the 5 questions under the heading 'Looking into the Story'. Then do 'My Own Story' solo (in private).

(Discussion, 20 Minutes) REGATHER as C-Groups and DISCUSS the questions and answers, especially focusing on questions 4 and 5 in 'Looking into the Story' and on questions 3, 4, and 5 in 'My Own Story'.

If you have time ask these two questions:

☐ How could Jesus help you with these problems?

☐ How could the story of Joseph help you to deal with these problems?

HELP the students understand clearly the secret of Joseph's success (trusting God, seeing things from his perspective) and the fact that God *wants* to help and *can* help them in their problems.

CLOSE with prayer in your C-Groups, remembering any needs that have been shared.

Optional Crowd Breakers

GUESS WHO?

This crowd breaker is great for C-Groups to compete against other C-Groups. Before the session, prepare a set of 8 stick-on name tags for each Group. The name tags can be: film stars, well-known athletes, comic strip or fictional characters—anyone that can be easily and quickly portrayed, such as:

☐ Bruce Forsyth

☐ Raquel Welch

☐ Romeo and Juliet

☐ Robin Day

☐ J. R.

☐ Margaret Thatcher

☐ Lady Godiva

☐ Tom and Jerry

☐ E.T.

While the leader is explaining the directions, have two helpers go to the C-Groups and put the name tags on each person—a different name tag for everyone in the Group.

On the word GO, one person in *each* C-Group turns around and lets the others in the Group see the name tag on his or her back. Then, the others start acting out (in silence) this character until the person can guess who it is.

Then the second person in the C-Group turns around and lets the others see the name tag. The others act out this character until the person can guess who it is, etc., until everyone in the group has guessed. The first C-Group to guess all the characters wins.

MATCH GAME (*For the whole youth group together*)
This is an indoor game that is quite simple and easy to play. Distribute a list similar to the following to each person:

1. Doughnut
2. A famous band
3. Looks like a foot
4. Headquarters
5. A stirring event
6. The end of winter
7. A pair of slippers
8. An old beau of mine
9. The peacemaker
10. Where love is found
11. Cause of the American revolution
12. Glass of water
13. A place for reflection
14. The reigning favourite
15. A morning caller
16. Fire when ready
17. Drive through the wood
18. Bound to shine
19. Life of China
20. Top dog
21. My native land

Next, place various articles on a table or around the room that will match the 'clues' given in the first list. For example, the corresponding items for the preceding list would be:

1. The letter 'o' on a card
2. Rubber band
3. Ruler
4. Pillow
5. Spoon
6. Letter 'r'
7. Two banana peels
8. Old ribbon bow
9. Pair of scissors
10. Dictionary
11. Tacks on tea bags
12. Blotter or sponge
13. Mirror
14. Umbrella
15. Alarm clock
16. Match
17. Nail
18. Shoe polish
19. Rice
20. Hot dog
21. Handful of earth

Of course, you may think of many more besides these. The winner is the person who can correctly match up all the items in the shortest time. To make the game harder, place twice as many items on the table than you have clues for.

 **GOING FURTHER**
C-Groups/25–30
Minutes

About Me . . . and My Problems

If you have time, ENCOURAGE the partners to work together on the Further study as well. The prayer that concludes the Further study is a very honest one. CAUTION partners that they are to take these prayers seriously and be an encouragement to their partner's success in overcoming the problem.

REGATHER with your C-Group and DISCUSS what each person learned from the Further study.

LEADERS' CHECKLIST

BEFORE THE SESSION

☐ Student Books: Enough for everyone? If the group members took them home, phone and remind them to bring them back.

☐ Meal: Is someone preparing the food?

☐ Crowd Breakers: Select one or two crowd breakers—something to start off the meeting and something to bring the C-Group together.

☐ Absentees: Ask the C-Group leaders to contact those of their Group who were absent last week.

☐ Research: Read the story of Joseph in the book of Genesis.

DURING THE SESSION

☐ Welcome: Welcome newcomers. Give them books. Write names on page 1.

☐ C-Group: Get together in Groups before the Warm-Up Exercise so that partners are chosen within their own C-Group.

☐ Partners: All exercises are worked on by partners before sharing with their C-Group.

☐ Model: Before any sharing experience, you go first . . . and set an example of honesty and openness.

AFTER THE SESSION

☐ Student Books: Collect the books unless you are assigning the Further study as homework.

☐ Evaluation: Get together with your Youth Worker Team and evaluate the session.

☐ Order: Order more Student Books.

☐ Retreat: Think about a retreat to close the course.

Session 5
My Values

Objective: To understand better what our values are; to examine our values in the light of Jesus' teachings on what's important; to make some lifestyle changes relating to values.

Setting: Room large enough for large group games with a cosy corner for C-Groups when they settle down for sharing.

Time: From 50 minutes to 2½ hours

- ☐ Meal/40 Minutes*
- ☐ Crowd Breakers/30 Minutes*
- ☐ C-Group Warm-Up/15 Minutes
- ☐ Starter Bible Study/30–35 Minutes
- ☐ Going Further/25–30 Minutes*

*Optional

If you have only 50 minutes, move to the C-Group Warm-Up immediately. If you have 2½ hours, the Further study can be incorporated into the regular meeting time. If not, you can assign this as homework for those interested in pursuing the subject further. For an older, or more mature group, you can condense the time required for the Starter Bible Study and spend more time on the Further study as a group.

Materials required:

- ☐ Student Books
- ☐ Pens
- ☐ Special Equipment for Crowd Breakers

Meal: If you are planning a meal, make sure you've contacted a mum or dad to bring the food and you've told the group members how much money they need to bring.

Crowd Breakers: Choose one or two. Some are for large groups and some are for the C-Group.

Review: If you assigned the Further study for homework, take a few moments and ask what the young people got out of their study.

WARM-UP
C-Groups/15
Minutes

Values Auction

WELCOME the group.
DISTRIBUTE the Student Books and pens and then nonchalantly announce that you will also be giving £1000 to each student.
BEGIN to hand out £1000 in play money to everyone. (You may use money from Monopoly or other table games or make your own.)

ASK everyone to turn to Session 5 in their books, and look over the list of items in the 'Values Auction'. EXPLAIN that they can bid on all of the items, but they can only spend £1000.

(Preparation, 3 Minutes) In silence, ASK everyone to jot down in the left column how much of their £1000 they want to bid on each item. (YOU HAVE TO BID ON AT LEAST 5 ITEMS.) ENCOURAGE them to plan their budget carefully.

TELL them that they do not have to stick to their budget when the bidding starts, but they should at least plan a budget to make sure they know what they want and about how much they are willing to spend—like any good business person. ALLOW about 3 minutes in silence for planning the budget.)

(Auction, 10 Minutes) GET TOGETHER in your C-Groups. The leader of each Group will be the auctioneer. The auctioneer should start the bidding on the first item at £50. 'Who will give me £50 for season tickets to your favourite sports team? . . . Who'll make it £60? . . . £70?' etc. (The C-Group leader can also enter into the bidding.)

You can revise your budget if you want to. And you can use any money that you budgeted for one item that you did not win.

The auctioneer can invent all sorts of sentimental stories to raise the value of an item (e.g., 'Cliff Richard will be on the holiday too'.) When the bidding finally stops on the first item, the person who 'won' it jots down the price they had to pay for the item in the RIGHT COLUMN . . . and gives the auctioneer that amount of Monopoly money.

Then the auctioneer starts the bidding on the next item at £50.

When all 15 items have been auctioned, ASK how many people didn't buy anything and/or still have money. ASK them if they'd like to bid for something now . . . or keep their money. Maybe someone would be willing to sell something they 'won' for a better price. Do the supplementary auction for a few minutes to allow some people to spend or keep their money.

When the auction is over, ASK them to DISCUSS in their C-Groups the two questions at the bottom.

STARTER BIBLE STUDY
C-Groups/30–35 Minutes

The Rich Young Ruler

To the total group, SAY something like, 'I have asked (name) to read a familiar passage of the Bible as we move into our Bible study on values.'

(Preparation, 15 Minutes) After Luke 18:18–25 has been read, ENCOURAGE them to pick a partner from their own C-Group and work on the questions in 'Looking into the Story'. Then work solo (alone) on the questions in 'My Own Story'. Allow them about 15 minutes for this.

(Discussion, 15 Minutes) REGATHER in C-Groups and DISCUSS the questions and answers. Quickly SKIM the 'Looking into the Story' and concentrate on 'My Own Story' questions 1, 2, 4, 5, and 7. Really ENCOURAGE your Group members to think of a plan for living out God's values at home and at school/college/work.

CLOSE by asking each one to pray for the person on their right.

GOING FURTHER
C-Groups/25–30 Minutes

About Me . . . and My Values

If you have time, ENCOURAGE the partners that worked together this session to get together and work on the questions in the Further study. Then, REGATHER in C-Groups to discuss what you discovered.

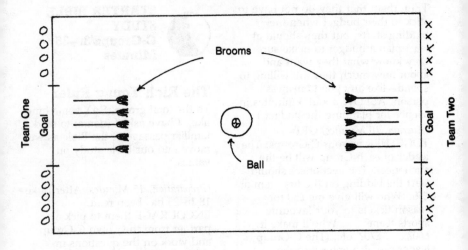

Optional Crowd Breakers

BROOM HOCKEY

This game may be played with as many as 30 or as few as 5 per team, but only 5 or 6 are actually on the field at one time from each team. Two teams compete by (at a whistle) running out onto the field, grabbing their brooms and swatting a volleyball placed in the centre through the opposite goal. Each team has a 'goalie', as in ice hockey or soccer, who can grab the ball with his hands and throw it back onto the playing field. If the ball goes out of bounds, the referee throws it back in. The ball may not be touched with hands, or kicked; but only hit with the broom. Score 1 point for each time the ball passes between the goal markers.

For a team with 30 members, for example, have them number off by sixes, which would give you 6 teams of 5 members each. Let all the 'ones' play a 3-minute period, then the 'twos', etc.

HAPPY HANDFUL RELAY (For two or three teams)

This relay may be easily adapted for indoor or outdoor use. Assemble two identical sets of at least 12 miscellaneous items (i.e., 2 brooms, 2 balls, 2 saucepans, 2 toilet rolls, 2 ladders, etc.) Use your imagination to collect an interesting variety of identical pairs of objects. Place the two sets of objects on two separate tables.

Line up a team for each table. The first player for each team runs to his table, picks up one item of his choice, runs back to his team, and passes the item to the second player. The second player carries the first item back to the table, picks up another item, and carries both items back to the third player. Each succeeding player carries the items collected by his teammates to the table, picks up one new item and carries them all back to the next player. The game will begin rapidly, but the pace will slow as each player decides which item to add to a growing armload of items. It will also take increasingly longer for one player to pass his burden to the next player in line.

Once picked up, an item may not touch the table or floor. Any item which is dropped in transit or transfer must be returned to the table by the leader. No one may assist the giving and receiving players in the exchange of items except through advice. The first team to empty its table wins.

MUSICAL HATS

Give a hat to everyone in the room. Ask them to put it on and stand in a circle. This game is played like 'musical chairs', but instead of a missing chair, there is a missing hat.

When the whistle blows, everyone starts walking in a circle. With their right hand ONLY, they grab the hat on the head of the person in front of them and place the hat on their head. When the whistle blows again, the person without a hat on their head is OUT.

The object of the game is to keep a hat on your head by grabbing the hat on the head of the person in front of you and putting it on your head.

You cannot use your left hand. You cannot hold your hat on your head. All you can do is to take the hat off of the head of the person in front of you and put their hat on your head.

Now, to start, get into a circle. Turn right . . . and start walking. (Leader: Remove one hat from the group after each round so that there is always one hat less than people. After each round, ask the person without a hat to step out.)

APPLE THROW *(For small groups)*

This is a simple but exciting game for small groups. The group is seated in chairs preferably in a closed circle. One person stands inside the circle. The group passes or throws an apple around the circle (to anyone in the circle they choose). The person in the middle then tries to touch the person who has the apple. When he catches someone with the apple, the two exchange positions. Also, if he catches the apple in mid air, the one who threw it has to exchange positions and become 'it', and the game is resumed.

LEADERS' CHECKLIST

BEFORE THE SESSION

☐ Student Books: Do you have enough?

☐ Meal: Do you have this taken care of?

☐ Crowd Breakers: Select one or two crowd breakers—something to start off the meeting and something to bring each C-Group together.

☐ Absentees: Ask the C-Group leaders to contact anyone from their group who was absent last week.

☐ Team Training: Keep getting together with your team as a support group.

DURING THE SESSION

☐ Welcome: Welcome newcomers. Give them books. Write their names on page 1.

☐ C-Groups: Get together as Groups before the Warm-Up exercise so auction is in C-Groups.

☐ Partners: Be sure to mix up the pairs that work on the Starter Bible Study together.

☐ Model: The leader always goes first on sharing—setting an example of candour and honesty.

AFTER THE SESSION

☐ Student Books: Collect the books unless you are assigning the Further study as homework.

☐ Evaluation: Get together with your team and evaluate the session.

☐ Order: Order more Student Books.

☐ Retreat: If possible, have an overnight special event for everyone at the close of the course.

Session 6
My Faith

Objectives: To continue to be a loving, caring, sharing community; to learn to 'walk by faith' through a trust walk; to explore the concept of faith and discover the growing edge of your faith.

Setting: Plenty of room for the crowd breakers and a cosy corner for the C-Groups to meet in comfort and intimacy.

Time: From 50 minutes to 2½ hours

- ☐ Meal/40 Minutes*
- ☐ Crowd Breakers/30 Minutes*
- ☐ C-Group Warm-Up/12–15 minutes
- ☐ Starter Bible Study/30–35 Minutes
- ☐ Going Further/25–30 Minutes*

*Optional

If you have only 50 minutes, move to the C-Group Warm-Up immediately. If you have 2½ hours, the Further study can be incorporated into the regular meeting time. If not, you can assign this as homework for those interested in pursuing the subject further. For an older, or more mature group, you can condense the time required for the Starter Bible Study and spend more time on the Further study as a Group.

Materials required:

- ☐ Student Books
- ☐ Pens
- ☐ Blindfolds for each pair in trust walk
- ☐ Special Equipment for Crowd Breakers
- ☐ Bibles for the Further study

Meal: If you're planning a meal, make sure you've contacted a mum or dad to bring the food and that you've told your whole group how much money they need to bring.

Crowd Breakers: Choose one or two. Some are for the large group and some are for the C-Groups.

Review: If you assigned the Further study for homework, take a few moments and ask what they got out of their study.

 WARM UP C-Groups/12–15 Minutes

Trust Walk

In advance, DETERMINE the general area for the 'trust walk'. If you're confined totally to one room, SET UP an obstacle course with tables, chairs, etc. Better still, allow the young people to walk through the building, or even outside, if weather permits.

WELCOME the group. DISTRIBUTE the books and pens. ASK each person to pair off with someone from their C-Group. EXPLAIN the trust walk. SAY something like: 'In a few minutes each of you is going to have an opportunity to walk by faith—to go on a "trust walk"—where you will be led blindfolded by your partner. You will be forced to trust him or her.' EXPLAIN the boundaries for the walk and TELL them that they will have 3 minutes to walk—one of you blindfolded and the other the leader. Then, after 3 minutes, you will reverse the roles and try it the other way around.

GIVE each set of partners a blindfold and send them on their way. After 3 minutes, blow a whistle and ask the pairs to reverse roles.

REGATHER in your C-Groups and DISCUSS these questions.

☐ How would you describe the inner feelings that you had on the trust walk?
☐ What was the worst moment for you during your trust walk?
☐ How would you describe your partner if this was the only time you'd done anything together?
☐ What did you discover about yourself during this time?
☐ What experience out of your past did this trust walk bring to mind?

 STARTER BIBLE STUDY C-Groups/30–35 Minutes

Thomas, An Honest Doubter

In advance, SELECT someone to read the Bible passage on 'Thomas, the Honest Doubter'. Before the person reads, briefly ASK the group what they know about Thomas. Then have the person read the passage.

(Preparation, 8 Minutes) Within your C-Groups, pair off again and ASK partners to work together on the Inner Feelings Scale and the Diary. (Allow about 8 minutes for this.)

(Discussion, 15 Minutes) REGATHER in your Groups and share your responses to the Inner Feelings

Scale and the Diary. Then DISCUSS the 5 questions for C-Groups. (Keep the discussion here to 15 minutes.) In the discussion, STRESS these two points:

☐ Thomas had good cause to doubt the disciples' report. They were emotionally upset at the time and, after all, they were saying that they had seen someone who was known to be dead. But when Jesus answered his doubting, Thomas accepted the proof and declared Jesus to be his Lord and his God.

☐ Thomas needed *visible* proof that Jesus has risen from the dead but Jesus said that we who believe without seeing him are more blessed. The apostle John reminds us that we have the Bible to tell us about Jesus' life, death, and resurrection. On the basis of this written account, John says, we should believe.

Don't stress these two points in such a way that people are afraid to reveal their doubts. As you instruct them to move to 'My Own Story' section, ENCOURAGE them to be honest in their responses.

(Preparation/Discussion, 6–8 Minutes) PAUSE for a moment to allow everyone to fill out 'My Own Story' in silence. Then, REGATHER in C-Groups to share what for them was the easiest area to believe . . . and what was the toughest.

(Note to Group Leaders: If possible, schedule some time alone with each member of your C-Group and go over their responses to 'My Own Story'. This will give them an opportunity to have some of their tough questions answered and it will give you a chance to minister personally to them and to get to know them better.)

61

GOING FURTHER
C-Groups/25–30 Minutes

About Me . . . and My Faith

If you have time, ENCOURAGE the partners to work together on the Further study and to work solo on the Personal Application.

Regather and DISCUSS the results in your C-Groups.

Optional Crowd Breakers

BUZZ-FIZZ
In your C-Groups, count up to 50 as fast as you can, but instead of saying *'five'* or any multiple of *'five'*, say *'Buzz'*. Instead of saying *'seven'* or any multiple of *'seven'*, say *'FIZZ'*.

For example, each person, in turn around the group, will sound off with *'one'* . . . *'two'* . . . *'three'* . . . *'four'* . . . and the next person will say *'BUZZ'*; the next person *'six'* and the next person *'FIZZ'*, etc.

If the number is a multiple of *'five'* and *'seven'*, say *'BUZZ-FIZZ'*. If you make a mistake, start again. The first C-Group to reach 50 wins.

ELECTRICITY (For two teams)
Divide the group into two equal groups. Have each group sit in a line, holding hands, with their backs facing the other group. A leader at one end spins a coin. If it is heads, the two students at the end send a signal down the line by squeezing the person's hand next to him. When the person at the other end

gets his hand squeezed he grabs the towel that is sitting between him and the end person on the other team. The team that grabs the towel first wins. If the coin comes up tails, then nothing is supposed to happen. Sometimes one of the teams will jump the gun and end up grabbing the towel even though it came up tails.

DOG-PATCH OLYMPICS (For C-Groups.)
Here's a chance to put on an international Olympic Games, with each C-Group entering a team. Here are some possible events:

- ☐ Discus throw (paper plate)
- ☐ Javelin (plastic straws)
- ☐ 200-foot crawl relay (4 team members crawling 50 feet backwards—on all fours—carrying the baton—toilet roll—in their mouth)
- ☐ Potato sack hop relay (4 on each team)
- ☐ Egg toss (winner is the twosome that throws the farthest distance to partner without breaking the egg)
- ☐ Piggyback relay
- ☐ Wheelbarrow race relay

Each C-Group has to enter one or more people or teams in each event. Winner of each event gets 10 points, runner-up team gets 5 points.

DUCKIE WUCKIE
Everyone sits in a circle on the floor with one person standing in the middle. The person in the middle is blindfolded and given a rolled-up newspaper. Then spin this person around while everyone else changes places. The blindfolded person finds a lap by using the end of the newspaper. This person then sits in the lap and says, 'Duckie Wuckie.' In a disguised voice the person being sat upon responds with 'quack-quack.' The blindfolded person tries to guess the identity of the voice (who the person is). If he/she is wrong, this blindfolded person is led to the centre of the group and spun around again for another try. If this person is right in their guess, this person changes places with the person they guessed.

LEADERS' CHECKLIST

BEFORE THE SESSION

☐ Bibles: Everyone needs a Bible for 'Going Further'.

☐ Student Books: Do you have enough?

☐ Meal: Do you have someone preparing it?

☐ Crowd Breakers: Choose one or two and collect the materials you need.

☐ Absentees: Ask C-Group leaders to contact members of their Group that were absent last week.

☐ Team Training: Go over the Bible study with your team.

DURING THE SESSION

☐ Welcome: Welcome newcomers. Give them books. Write their names on page 1.

☐ Trust Walk: Use the trust walk instead of crowd breakers.

☐ Partners: Mix up the pairs who work together.

☐ Model: Share your answers first before you ask the Groups to share. Encourage honesty by giving honest answers yourself.

AFTER THE SESSION

☐ Collect: Collect the Student Books.

☐ Evaluate: Get together with your Youth Worker Team and evaluate the session.

☐ Celebration: Plan something special to conclude the course next week. If you are planning a party, ask group members to bring refreshments.

Session 7
My Tomorrow

Objectives: To *complete* the course successfully; to *be* a loving, caring, sharing community to one another; to *determine* whether you are part of the 'harvest field' or part of the 'work force' in the sharing of the Good News of Jesus Christ; to *evaluate* your growth during this course.

Setting: Casual, informal atmosphere with movable chairs that can be changed into a worship setting if you decide to conclude this course with worship.

Time: From 50 minutes to 2½ hours

☐ Meal/40 Minutes*
☐ C-Group Warm-Up/5–7 Minutes*
☐ Starter Bible Study/25–30 Minutes
☐ Summing-Up Exercise/20 Minutes
☐ Worship/Open-ended*
*Optional

If you have only 50 minutes, move to the C-Group Warm-Up immediately. If you have 2½ hours, the special Summing-Up Exercise may be incorporated into the regular meeting time.

Also, you may wish to conclude the course with worship together or a general sharing time. Special instructions for these options are given on the next page.

Materials required:

☐ Student Books
☐ Pens
☐ Special Materials for the Closing Celebration

Leadership: At the team meeting, discuss the options for concluding this course with something special.

Meal: If you're planning a meal, make sure you've contacted a mum or dad to bring the food and that you've told the whole group how much money they need to bring.

Review: If you assigned the Further study last week for homework, take a few moments to let group members share what they learned.

 **WARM-UP
C-Groups/5–7
Minutes**

Job Centre
WELCOME the group. ASK them to move immediately to their C-Groups and work on the Job Centre exercise.

(Group leaders: Think about your Group in advance. In light of the uniqueness of each member of your Group, you may want to invent a couple more positions—headmaster, cook, etc.—with descriptions to toss out during the course of the discussion.)

ENCOURAGE your Group to read, silently, the description of each position, jotting down the names of the others in their C-Group as they find a special place for each Group member. Then get together as a C-Group. ASK one person to sit in silence while the others EXPLAIN where they put this person's name and why. Then ASK the next person to sit in silence while the others explain

what they chose for this person. Use this exercise to AFFIRM what you have found unique and valuable in one another.

 STARTER BIBLE STUDY C-Groups/25–30 Minutes

Workers and Harvest

SAY something like: 'This is the last session of this course. We are focusing on the theme of "My Tomorrow" and the big question is: Where do we go from here? We've looked at our specialness, our interests, abilities, problems, values, and faith. With these in mind, we're going to look at our future. I've asked (name) to read our Bible study passage.'

(Preparation, 8–10 Minutes) After Matthew 10:35–38 has been read, ASK them to work with a partner from their C-Group on the 'Looking into the Story' questions. Then work solo on the 'My Own Story' questions.

(Discussion, 20 Minutes) REGATHER in C-Groups and DISCUSS the questions. Get responses on all the questions but focus especially on questions 4 and 5 in 'Looking into the Story'. Make sure it's clear who the workers are and what it means to harvest.

Question 1 in 'My Own Story' is very personal. But after 7 weeks of caring and sharing within C-Groups everyone should feel free to share where they are.

Cover all four questions in 'My Own Story' but focus on questions 1 and 4.

 **SUMMING UP C-Groups/20 Minutes**

Tying Up Loose Ends

SAY something like, 'Now we've finished the session we may need some time to reflect on what we've learned during this course.'

(5 Minutes) TURN back to the front of your books and place an 'x' on the diagram representing where you are right now with God. Then REGATHER with your C-Group and explain where you put your 'x' and why.

(15 Minutes) Then TURN to the 'Summing-Up' questionnaire at the back of the book and SHARE your answer to question 1. If you have time left over, go around your Group a second time, on question 2—and so on, until you have either gone through the questionnaire or run out of time.

(Note: The answers to these questions and to number 1 of 'My Own Story' can give you great insight into where the students are. Use this information to accomplish one of the major goals of the course: to help people respond to Jesus Christ. If you detect that any of your C-Group members are sincerely questioning or seriously floundering, make an appointment to see them and talk it over.)

CLOSING
All Together/Open-ended

To celebrate your experience during this course, here are two options:

Quaker Service: This is sometimes called a 'testimonial' meeting.

Move to a quiet, meditative place, such as the chancel in the church . . . or turn out the lights and light a fire . . . or candles. Begin the service by explaining a little about the Quaker tradition and the importance of being in silence . . . letting God speak to us before we speak to him or to others.

To introduce the period of silence, lead the group in singing together a meditative hymn or chorus to focus the attention. Then wait in silence until someone breaks the silence with their sharing.

Suggest that the sharing be limited to the 'next steps' in their spiritual journey . . . and where they need the support of the community in their venture.

Set the pace with your own example. Make it personal, very specific . . . and honest.

Commissioning Service. Change the atmosphere in the room or move to another place. This service is best carried out in small clusters—with people that know each other.

Give each person in the group a chance to explain the 'next step' in their life . . . or what 'God is asking me to do'. Then have this person kneel or sit in the centre of the group while the others in the group commission this person to the task they have explained, one person praying for the whole group while everyone 'lays their hands' on the head or shoulders.

Then the next person explains where they need to move out . . . and kneels in the group to be commissioned, etc., until everyone has been commissioned.

X-CERTIFICATE:

On Moral Questions

1 **STARTING POINT**
Acts 4:1–3, 13–20

2 **TEMPTING CHOICES**
Matthew 4:1–11

3 **YOUR MIND MATTERS**
Romans 12:2

4 **CONTROLLING THE ALMIGHTY TONGUE**
James 3:3–6, 8, 10–11

5 **SEX, SEX, AND MORE SEX**
Genesis 1:27–28, 31

6 **HONESTY AND INTEGRITY**
Proverbs 6:16–19, 8:5–9, 13a

7 **FORGIVENESS**
Luke 15:11–32

'Don't let the world around you squeeze you into its own mould, but let God re-mould your minds from within, so that you may prove in practice that the plan of God for you is good, meets all his demands and moves towards the goal of true maturity.'
Romans 12:2 (Phillips Translation)

CONTENTS

WARM-UP

to build trust and confidence in the C-Groups before the Bible study

STARTER BIBLE STUDY

to share 'my own story' in the C-Groups through a Bible story

GOING FURTHER

to go deeper into the Bible

---

1 STARTING POINT

My Coat of Arms
Take a few minutes and using a coat of arms explain the 'moral roots' you bring to this course.

Who's in Charge Here?
The authorities arrest Peter and John, throw them in jail, and tell them to stop talking about Jesus. But the authorities aren't the authority in the disciples' lives. The Lord is in charge. Acts 4:1–20.

Two for the Price of One
Jesus is both Saviour and Lord. What does that mean in your life?

---

2 TEMPTING CHOICES

Magazine Rack Raid
Flip through some magazines, pick out some adverts and analyse what they promise. How do the mass media tempt you?

Tempting Choices for Jesus
The devil goes after Jesus and loses. Can you win, too? Here are some principles for victory. Matthew 4:1–11.

How to Beat the Opposition
See the strategies of Satan and develop tactics for defeating the temptations that come your way.

---

3 YOUR MIND MATTERS

The Critic's Choice
Evaluate the eight most popular programmes on television and ask some personal questions about them and how they affect your mind and the minds of others.

How to Be a Nonconformist
God tells us we are to be nonconformists in society and that nonconformity begins with the mind. Find out how from Romans 12:1–2.

Reprogramming the Mind
Be specific. Determine, through the Word of God, how to change your mind.

On Moral Questions

4 CONTROLLING THE TONGUE

Hot Seat
Write down what you'd probably say in a variety of situations and then see how well members of your C-Group know you.

Tongue: Tamed or Troublesome?
James says the tongue when untamed is a heap of trouble. Evaluate yours and build some new speech patterns. James 3:3–11.

Tongue: Trained or Terrible?
Using the book of Proverbs, read more about the tongue and sharpen your strategy for bringing yours under control.

5 SEX, SEX, AND MORE SEX

Ten Questions on Sex
Give your opinions about sex.

About Me ... and God's Gift of Sex
How does God view sex? Why did he create it? Why is sex outside of marriage wrong in God's sight? Does he care that you're sexually tempted? What can you do? Genesis 1; Mark 10:5–9; 1 Cor. 6.

Love and Sex
The physical and emotional. How do love and sex relate? What does God say? Summarise how you feel about this important subject.

6 HONESTY/ INTEGRITY

Lines of Extremes
Are you more like Top Cat or The Underdog? An unfinished Symphony or a Disco? Mother Teresa or Dame Edna? Who do the rest of your C-Group think you're like? What does all this have to do with integrity?

Wise Up
Wisdom, integrity, and honesty are interwoven . . . and all-important in God's sight . . . and crucial to maturity. What is integrity? Do you have any? Proverbs 6:16–19 and 8:5–9.

Steps to Honesty
James lists eight steps to honesty and integrity. Look at those. Examine areas in your life where you're struggling with honesty, and work with God and your C-Group in developing a plan for a life filled with integrity.

7 FORGIVENESS

Moments
Take a few moments to reflect on some memorable experiences in your life.

The Runaway
This runaway was a kid who had blown it and lived an X-Certificate life. He finally came to his senses and was desperately in need of forgiveness and acceptance. He got it. So can you. Luke 15:11–32.

Forgiveness as a Way of Life
Forgiveness is one of the most important concepts in all of the Bible for beginning and continuing the walk with Jesus Christ. Dive deep into the Word and understand and experience this great gift.

Session 1
Starting Point:
If Jesus Is Boss

Objectives: To get better acquainted with one another; to form C-Groups for the first time in the course; to help members of the group realise that they are special and that they are important to the group; to encourage everyone to make sure that Jesus is the boss of their life.

Setting: Casual, informal atmosphere—movable chairs or a rug on the floor—where the group can gather, have fun, and be relaxed.

Time: From 50 minutes to 2½ hours

☐ Meal/30–40 Minutes*
☐ Crowd Breakers 20–30 Minutes*
☐ C-Group Warm-Up/17–20 Minutes
☐ Starter Bible Study/35–40 Minutes
☐ Going Further/30–35 Minutes*
*Optional

If you have only 50 minutes, move to the C-Group Warm-Up immediately. If you have 2½ hours, the Further study can be incorporated into the regular meeting time. If not, you can assign this as homework for those interested in pursuing the subject in greater depth. For an older, or more mature group, you can condense the time required for the Starter Bible Study and spend more time on the Further study.

Materials required:

☐ Student Books
☐ Pens
☐ Special equipment for the optional Crowd Breakers you plan to use

Leadership: Look through the 'Leaders' Checklist'.

Meal: If you are planning a meal, make sure you've contacted a mum or dad for the food and told your group members how much money to bring (which goes to the parents to help cover the costs). Invest in some paper products—napkins, paper plates, and cups—to reduce washing-up.

Crowd Breakers: To start off the meeting, check page 73. There are some for the whole group together and some for small C-Groups—to help build camaraderie in a fun way. Make sure you have the equipment that is needed for any crowd breaker you choose.

INTRODUCTION
All Together/3 Minutes

Welcome

Welcome the group and INTRODUCE them to this new course. SAY something like: 'I want to welcome all of you here. For the next 7 weeks (or sessions), we're going to be involved in a course called X-CERTIFICATE, a study that looks at personal morality and how we can know and do what's right.' (DISTRIBUTE the Student Books and pens.) 'Open your book to the inside front cover. I'd like to review some of the subjects we'll be looking at over the next few weeks.'

GIVE them a quick overview, briefly touching on the topics for the next 7 sessions. Don't go into much detail; the purpose of the overview is to give them only a thumbnail sketch of what to expect and to whet their appetite.

CONTINUE with something like: 'Each week we'll begin with a warm-up exercise and then move to small C-Groups where we will be able to discuss these issues and learn some good stuff. Each C-Group will be made up of from 4 to 6 students (or whatever your number is for these groups) and one leader.' (READ off the names of the leaders of the C-Groups from the Youth Worker Team. Make sure there's room for those teenagers you didn't anticipate being involved but who are now here and ready to go.)

ASK them to join their C-Groups as you read the names. As soon as they've grouped, move immediately to the Warm-Up for the first session.

WARM-UP
C-Groups/17–20
Minutes

My Coat of Arms

(Part 1; 3 Minutes) INSTRUCT everyone to fill in their coat of arms on page 6. (GIVE an example of how you would fill in your coat of arms.)

(Part 2; 5 Minutes) ASK everyone to get together with one other person from their C-Group and explain their coat of arms. If there is time, ALLOW each person to respond to their partner with these sentences (give an example):

- ☐ I really like what you had to say about. . . .
- ☐ I didn't expect you to say. . . .
- ☐ I would like to know more about. . . .

(Part 3; 5 Minutes) REGROUP with your C-Group and GO around the circle. Let each person share the most interesting thing they learned about their partner. Simply finish the sentence: 'The most interesting thing I learned about my partner was. . . .'

(Part 4; 5 Minutes) TURN to 'BEFORE AND AFTER' at the front of the Student Book. SAY something like 'To get an idea of where we are, I'd like each of you to take this little survey. At the end of 7 weeks (or sessions), we'll do it again to see how far we've come or how far we've gone—whatever the case may be.' READ the directions and proceed. (Explain what a continuum is and give examples of where you would mark the survey.)

After everyone has finished the survey, ASK the group if they have any comments to make about the survey or about their marks. This is not a heavy discussion time, so if there are few comments, don't worry about it and move to the Starter Bible Study.

STARTER BIBLE
STUDY
C-Groups/35–40
Minutes

Who's in Charge Here?

MOVE to the Starter Bible Study. SAY something like: 'Now, let's begin our study on "Who's in charge?" '

In advance, select a student who is a good reader to read the Bible passage. (NEVER call on a person to read if you haven't checked with him/her before. For some students, who don't read aloud well, being called upon to read is a very humiliating and anxiety-producing experience.)

(*Open Discussion, 3 Minutes*) BEGIN by asking the group what they know about Peter and John. After you've heard some comments, SAY something like: 'In the story we are going to look at today, Peter has just healed a crippled beggar, an amazed crowd has gathered, and Peter and John are telling them about Jesus and his great power. The Jewish religious leaders become upset and make a move to silence Peter and John.'

(*Preparation, 8 Minutes*) Now, HAVE your reader read and then ASK the partners who were together in the Warm-Up exercise to get together again and work on the 'Looking into the Story' questions. Then, work for 2 or 3 minutes on your own on 'My Own Story'.

(*Discussion, 20 Minutes*) REGROUP in C-Groups and DISCUSS. Quickly move through the first seven questions, getting their answers and commenting a little on the story. On question 8, take more time. DISCUSS what being 'boss' means and what it must have meant to Peter and John to have God for their boss. TALK about how tough it must have been to go to prison (prison conditions were terrible) and to be constantly hassled when you were only trying to tell people what you'd seen. THE POINT: Jesus is the best boss anyone can have but that doesn't mean life will be easy. There are some choices to make that have tough consequences.

Then, FOCUS on 'My Own Story' questions. Go through them more slowly. Because it's the first session of the series, some people may be a bit hesitant to share. ENCOURAGE them and without monopolising the discussion, SHARE some of your answers to the questions in a very honest, transparent way—letting them know you have some of the same feelings they have.

Question 7 is important for them to understand. THE POINT: If you don't know who your boss is, you have no authority for making decisions and no power to help you do what you know is right. Once you discover who your boss is and what he has to say, you can begin to face the moral issues in your life.

CLOSE in prayer, thanking God for each member of the group (by name, if you know all their names) and committing the next six sessions to him, asking God to give everyone wisdom to know what to do and the courage and the power to do it.

 GOING FURTHER C-Groups/30–35 Minutes

Two for the Price of One

If you have time, ASK the Group members to work in pairs on the first three questions and alone on the last two and the thank-you letter.

Then, REGATHER and DISCUSS the questions and their answers. LISTEN to discover who is asking for specific help or who is a little confused or who wants to invite Christ to become Saviour and Lord of his or her life. MAKE a mental note (and maybe a pen and paper note later), and FOLLOW UP during the week with a visit in person or a phone call, so that you can help these teenagers take the next step of faith.

Optional Crowd Breakers

PASS THE FEETBALL

Give each group a large balloon. Blow up the balloon to the size of a watermelon.

By groups, sit in a circle with your feet in the middle. On the word go, pass the balloon around your group, using only your feet. (If it touches your hands, you have to start again.) The first group to pass the balloon *five* times around their group wins.

AUTOGRAPH HUNT

This is a great crowd breaker for parties or socials. Type up a copy of the list below for everyone in the group; however, no two lists should be in the same order unless the group is very large. The idea is to have everyone doing something different at the same time. Also, you are not able to tell who is winning until the game is over. The winner is the first one to complete all ten things on his list *in order*. Anyone who will not do what someones asks him to do is automatically disqualified.

1. Get ten different autographs. First and last names in full. (On the back of this sheet.)
2. Unlace someone's shoe, lace it, and tie it again. (Not your own.)
3. Get a hair over six inches long from someone's head. (Let them remove it.)
4. Get a girl to do a somersault and sign her name here. _____
5. Have a boy do five pushups for you and sign his name here. _____
6. Play 'Ring a ring of roses' with someone and sing out loud.
7. Do twenty-five jumps from 'at ease' to 'attention', and back again; saluting each time. Have someone count them for you. _____
8. Sing the National Anthem (first verse only).
9. Leapfrog over someone five times.
10. You were given a piece of bubble gum at the beginning of the race. Chew it up and blow ten bubbles. Find someone who will watch you do it and sign here when you have finished. _____

LEADERS' CHECKLIST

BEFORE THE SESSION

☐ Student Books and pens: Make sure you have enough.

☐ C-Group leaders: Make sure you have a leader for every 4 to 6 students.

☐ Meal: Get one of the mothers to prepare something to feed the group. Ask each person to bring the necessary amount of money.

☐ Crowd breakers: Pick one or two to start off the meeting. Get the special equipment required.

☐ Research: Read Acts 1–4 and be prepared to explain the background to the Starter Bible Study.

DURING THE SESSION

☐ C-Groups: The objective of this session is to establish C-Groups. Divide the youth group into C-Groups and put one member of the Youth Worker Team with each C-Group.

☐ Student Books: Distribute and ask students to write their names in the front.

☐ Welcome: Explain the course. Stress the need for regular attendance.

☐ Partners: The C-Group Warm-Up starts off in pairs. If there is an odd number, the C-Group leader drops out.

AFTER THE SESSION

☐ Collect: Collect the Student Books unless you are assigning the Further study as homework.

☐ C-Group leaders: Get together and evaluate the session. Ask the leaders to contact their group members during the week.

☐ Order: Order more Student Books.

Session 2
Tempting Choices

Objectives: To get better acquainted with one another; to understand the temptations Jesus faced and the tactics of Satan; to learn ways that we can better face temptation; to continue to build a learning, caring, loving, sharing community.

Time: From 50 minutes to 2½ hours

□ Meal/30–40 Minutes*
□ Crowd Breakers/20–30 Minutes*
□ C-Group Warm-Up/15–20 Minutes
□ Starter Bible Study/30–35 Minutes
□ Going Further/25–30 Minutes*
*Optional

If you have only 50 minutes, move to the C-Group Warm-Up immediately. If you have 2½ hours, the Further study can be incorporated into the regular meeting time. If not, you can assign this as homework for those interested in pursuing the subject. For an older, or more mature group, you can condense the time required for the Starter Bible Study and spend more time on the Further study.

Materials required:

□ Student Books
□ Pens
□ A pile of magazines (*not* Christian ones!)—including some general ones (e.g. *Punch, Vogue, Woman's Own*) and several teenage magazines.
□ Equipment for Crowd Breakers

Meal: If you are planning a meal, make sure you've contacted a mum or dad for the food and told the whole youth group how much money they need to bring.

Crowd Breakers: Select one or two of the crowd breakers. Some are for the whole group and some are for the small C-Groups. Collect the special equipment.

Review: If you assigned the Further study from session 1 for homework this past week, take a few moments and ask what they got out of the study.

WARM-UP
C-Groups/15–20 Minutes

Magazine Rack Raid

Note: This is a longer Warm-Up and serves as the springboard for the study and discussion on temptation.

WELCOME the troops. Ask them to turn to Session 2. DISTRIBUTE a pile of magazines to each C-Group. Make sure each group gets a varied assortment of magazines.

(Preparation, 10 Minutes) DIVIDE the C-Groups in half so that there are 2–3 people working together. GO OVER the process. They should quickly flip through the magazines and select some adverts that really stand out. Then, in their Student Book, they should pick four and analyse each one: (jotting down their findings in their books.)

- What does it promise?
- How does it relate to real life?
- How does the advert tempt/encourage/influence?
- Does the lifestyle presented by the advert agree with the biblical teachings on how a Christian should live?

LOOK beyond the product being sold to the hidden message the advert seems to convey (e.g., 'Well, they said *anything* could happen after a Smirnoff'). To help them understand the process, SHOW AND TELL an advert from a magazine and answer the four questions about this advert.

(Discussion, 10 Minutes) GIVE the groups 10 minutes to work on adverts. Then ASK the C-Groups to regather and DISCUSS their findings.

Finally, GO AROUND and ask each person to finish the sentence: 'One thing I learned from this analysis is. . . .'

STARTER BIBLE STUDY
C-Groups/30–35 Minutes

Tempting Choices for Jesus

MOVE to the Starter Bible Study by saying something like: 'Jesus didn't have the media and magazines bombarding him but he was confronted by the toughest tempter in the world, the devil himself.'

(Preparation, 15 Minutes) In advance, ASK a student to read the Bible passage. Have him/her do it now.

Then, ASK the C-Groups to divide into twos and work together on ALL of the questions, including 'My Own Story'. (At the 7-minute mark, TELL them they have about 8 minutes left and ENCOURAGE them to continue moving through the study.)

(Discussion, 10–15 Minutes) When they have completed the questions, REGROUP and DISCUSS. On the 'Looking into the Story' questions, concentrate on numbers 2, 9, and 10. On question 2, ASK your Group members: 'What's the longest time you ever went without food? Have you ever been alone in a desert?' etc. GET the point across that Jesus was hungry and probably tired. Satan tried to hit him when he was weak. STRESS the point that Satan doesn't quit. He just plans new strategy and waits for another opportunity. On question 9, note that God wanted Jesus to understand temptation and that because he does, we know that he understands what we're going through. SHARE Hebrews 4:15 with them.

On the 'My Own Story' questions, FOCUS on all of them but especially on 6, 7, and 8. Major points: there are different ways to pursue needs and wants (1); the Bible is very important in dealing with the devil (2–5); all of us are tempted in many areas; it's not a sin to be tempted (Jesus was); sin comes when we give in to temptation (6). Share the good news of 1 Corinthians 10:13. DISCUSS ways they've found to deal successfully with temptation (7–8).

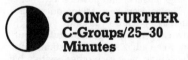

GOING FURTHER
C-Groups/25–30 Minutes

How to Beat the Opposition

If you have time, ASK the group to find a partner and work on questions 1–6 together, then the Personal Application on their own.

REGROUP and DISCUSS. Don't probe too deeply on anything they wrote in the Personal Application. But if anyone wants to share what

he/she is going to do, fine. ENCOURAGE each one to find one person who will pray for them this week.

Optional Crowd Breakers

LITTLE NEMO AND LITTLE NEMA

This is the old ventriloquist act in reverse. Instead of one person playing two roles, you have two people playing one role: (1) one person providing the heads and legs (with their arms) and (2) the other person (behind the sheet) providing the arms.

For this skit, you need (a) two people to play the boy and (b) two to play the girl. The second person stands behind the first person and reaches his or her arms around (under the sheet) to be the arms of the first person.

In addition, two others stand by as assistants to provide the materials and give advice.

AS THE SCENE OPENS: The scene takes place in Little Nemo's bathroom for the guy and Little Nema's bathroom for the girl.

The boy's assistant asks Little Nemo: 'You've got this date with Nema tonight. Do you think you ought to shave?' (Hand him the shaving cream . . . and then a bladeless razor.)

At the same time, the girl's assistant asks Little Nema: 'You've got this date tonight with Nemo. Do you think you ought to fix your face?' (Hand her some rouge, lipstick, and powder, etc.)

The advisers keep asking questions, such as: 'What do you think you ought to wear?' and giving them stuff to put on. Keep advising with questions until the couple meet each other—with a big kiss.

For even more fun, have a girl play the second person (behind the sheet) for Little Nemo and a guy play the second person (behind the sheet) for the girl. This will not only look weird, but will also provide a lot of laughs as they start to make up, get dressed, etc.

FRISBEE FOOTBALL (For two teams)

This game is a mixture of Frisbee and lacrosse. All that is needed is a playing field, a Frisbee, and from 10 to 75 players. Goals are set up on opposite ends of the field, by placing markers about ten feet apart. Divide up into two teams. Each team selects goalies, and perhaps other positions such as defender, attacker, forward, middle, back, etc. The two teams then line up on opposite ends of the field and the Frisbee is placed in the middle. On the starting whistle, players run for the Frisbee, and the first to get it may pass it to any other player on his team. When a player catches it, he may run with it, pass it, or down it, which stops the play for a free throw. (To down it, he simply falls on it.) Any player carrying the Frisbee may be 'tagged' (touched) by a member of the other team and must then surrender the Frisbee to him immediately. (Referees should make judgements on this.) If a player downs the Frisbee before being tagged, he can then stand up and throw it to any other player on his team without interference. However, once the Frisbee is thrown, it may be intercepted. Also, a person downing the Frisbee cannot score after downing it. Goals are scored by throwing the Frisbee between the goal markers.
Note: This can also be played with a balloon filled up with water. If the balloon breaks, the other team gets possession with a new balloon.

MIXED-UP RELAY *(For teams or C-Groups)*

This is a different kind of relay race in which each contestant does something different. What the contestants do is determined by the directions in a bag at the other end of the relay course.

At the beginning of the race, each team is lined up single file as usual. On a signal, the first person in each team runs to the other end of the course to a chair. On the chair is a bag containing instructions written on separate pieces of paper. The contestant draws out one of the instructions, reads it, and follows it as quickly as possible. Before returning to the team, the contestant must tag the chair. The contestant then runs back and tags the next runner. The relay proceeds in this manner and the team that uses all of its instructions first is the winner. Below are a few examples of directions:

1. Run around the chair 5 times while continuously yelling, 'The Yankees are coming, the Yankees are coming.'
2. Stand on one foot while holding the other in your hand, tilt your head back, and count, '10, 9, 8, 7, 6, 5, 4, 3, 2, 1, Blast Off!'
3. Take your shoes off, put them on the wrong foot, and then tag your nearest opponent.
4. Go to the person at the back of your team, make 3 different 'funny-face' expressions, then return to the chair before tagging your next runner.
5. Put your hands over your eyes and snort like a pig 5 times and meow like a cat 5 times.
6. Sit in the chair, fold your arms, and laugh hard and loud for 5 seconds.
7. Run around the chair backwards 5 times while clapping your hands.

LEADERS' CHECKLIST

BEFORE THE SESSION

- ☐ Magazines: Collect a huge pile of magazines for the Warm-Up.

- ☐ C-Groups: Have each C-Group leader contact the members of his/her group.

- ☐ Meal: Contact person in charge of the meal.

- ☐ Crowd breakers: Choose two or three to collect the materials you need.

- ☐ Team: Meet and go over the plan for the meeting.

DURING THE SESSION

- ☐ Welcome: Welcome newcomers. Give out the Student Books. Write their names inside. Assign newcomers to a C-Group.

- ☐ Warm-Up: Note the C-Groups split in half to work on the exercise. Then, regather to discuss.

- ☐ Model: Before any sharing experience, you *go first*. Set the pace for openness and honesty. Give personal examples to explain instructions.

AFTER THE SESSION

- ☐ Evaluation: Get together with your C-Group leaders and evaluate the session.

- ☐ Student Books: Collect the books, unless you have assigned the Further study for homework.

- ☐ Order: Order more books for newcomers.

- ☐ Social: Plan something special for about halfway through the course, and an overnight special/retreat at the close.

Session 3
Your Mind Matters

Objective: To get better acquainted with one another; to check Session 2's 'temptation strategy'; to realise the importance of the mind in moral choices; to learn how to have the mind transformed and renewed; to continue to build a learning, caring, sharing community.

Time: From 50 minutes to 2½ hours

- ☐ Meal/30–40 Minutes*
- ☐ Crowd Breakers/25–30 Minutes*
- ☐ C-Group Warm-Up/10–12 Minutes
- ☐ Starter Bible Study/40–45 Minutes
- ☐ Going Further/30–35 Minutes*
*Optional

If you have only 50 minutes, move to the C-Group Warm-Up immediately. If you have 2½ hours, the Further study can be incorporated into the regular meeting time. If not, you can assign this as homework for those interested in pursuing the subject. For an older, or more mature group, you can condense the time required for the Starter Bible Study and spend more time on the Further study.

Materials required:

- ☐ Student Books
- ☐ Pens
- ☐ *Radio Times* and *TV Times* (can be a few weeks old)
- ☐ Special equipment for crowd breakers

Leadership: Review the 'Leaders' Checklist'.

Meal: If you are planning on a meal, make sure you've contacted a mum or dad for the food and that you've told your group members how much money they need to bring.

Crowd Breakers: Select one or two. Some are for the group all together and some are for the small C-Groups.

Review: If you assigned the Further study as homework in session 2, you may want to talk about it before you move to the C-Group Warm-Up for this session. Assess your time, and plan your schedule accordingly if you wish to add a discussion of the Further study of the last session.

**WARM-UP
C-Groups/10–12
Minutes**

The Critic's Choice
WELCOME the group. Immediately ASK them to join their C-Groups. In the C-Groups, REVIEW the temptation strategies devised in the Further study or Starter Bible Study in session 2. These are some of the questions you might ask: How did it go? How successful were you? What did you learn that you might try this week?

(Preparation, 5 Minutes) TURN to Session 3 in the Student Book. DIVIDE the C-Group into twos. GIVE each twosome a *Radio Times* or *TV Times*.

ASK each twosome to jot down in their Student Books a list of the ten most popular TV programmes and CODE their list with the codes given in their Student Books.

(Discussion, 5 Minutes) REGATHER in C-Groups and PRESENT your top ten programmes and how you coded these programmes. Then, DISCUSS the four questions under 'C-Group Discussion Questions' in the Student Books.

 STARTER BIBLE STUDY C-Groups/40–45 Minutes

How to Be a Nonconformist

BEGIN by asking the question, 'What does the mind have to do with moral choices—the subject of our entire series?' SAY something like 'The mood of our day is characterised by ideas, lifestyles, and philosophies of life that contradict what Jesus Christ had to say about living. Materialism (the pursuit of money), pragmatism (if it works, do it), and humanism (man at the centre of the universe, man can make it without God) are only three of many philosophies that compete for our attention. Evidences of people living apart from God's way of life can be seen in literature, television and films, dress styles, lifestyles, speech, etc. The way people live reflects what's inside of them. A wise man in the Old Testament said, "As a man thinks, so is he" (Proverbs 23:7). Your mind and how you think is very important for how you live and act. That may be why there are so many references in the Bible to your mind and thought life. Computer programmers refer to the

GIGO principle—Garbage In, Garbage Out. That means if you feed the computer wrong information, it will spit out nothing but useless information.' Then, CALL ON the person you've chosen in advance to read the Bible passage. EMPHASISE that this verse gives a *command*. It's not an *option* for Christians. We need to take it seriously and see what it means in daily living.

(Preparation, 15–20 Minutes) GET BACK with your partner from the Warm-Up exercise and work together on the 'Looking into the Story' questions. ENCOURAGE them to look at every possible answer for every question and to decide carefully which answer fits. CHALLENGE them to fill in the 'Other: _____' option too.

After 5–7 minutes, BREAK IN and INSTRUCT them to work solo on the questions under 'My Own Story'. Note: This is a tougher study than the past two in 'My Own Story'. MINGLE with your Group, helping them with questions they're having difficulty with and encouraging them to think and write.

(Discussion, 20–25 Minutes) REGATHER in C-Groups and SPEND the remaining time in discussion. COVER all the questions but concentrate more on question 4 on the 'Looking into the Story' section and 2, 3, 4, 5, 6, 7, and 8 in 'My Own Story'. TRY TO really give them an understanding of what it means to be transformed and how important it is for them to be willing to allow God to transform their minds. At the conclusion of the discussion, ASK, 'How can we as C-Group members help one another in this transformation process?' BRAINSTORM and then come up

with a plan. Maybe the group members want to be held accountable for how much TV they watch and how much time they spend on God's Word. If so, have partners check with one another during the week, etc. USE your creativity in putting together a 'Mind Renewal Plan' for the C-Group.

CLOSE in prayer, entrusting to God the success of the plan.

 GOING FURTHER
C-Groups/30–35 Minutes

Programming the Mind

If possible, let the C-Group work again in pairs on everything but the Personal Application. They should work solo on this. Then, regather and DISCUSS questions 1–6 and ask members to share with their partners the one step they want to take to reprogramme their mind (the third half-finished sentence in Personal Application). Partners will then hold each other accountable.

Note: This Further study can be very helpful. If you don't have time to do it as a group, assign it as a homework project. Then, late in the week, phone every member of your C-Group and see how they have done on the Further study and what questions they have, etc. If they need to be held accountable on the three steps, ENCOURAGE them to phone their partners and set up this accountability.

Optional Crowd Breakers

BODY PAINTING

Ask a boy from each C-Group to volunteer as the models for a body-painting contest. The rest of the C-Group are the designers. They must create a huge hat to fit over the shoulders of their model—covering up the head and arms. Then, on the bare chest of the boy they have to draw two eyes, a nose, and a mouth—using the natural 'features' on his chest for starters. Then, cover the hips with a coat or sheet to appear like shoulders.

Give each C-Group 5 minutes to create their 'body painting' before the 'judging' by someone for the most creative sculpture.

For paint, you can use liquid shoe polish, wide felt-tip pens (*water* based), or washable poster paint and brushes.

CHINESE PING-PONG (*For two teams*)
About ten or so people stand around a ping-pong table, one on each end, the rest on the sides. The first person serves the ball over the net to the one on the other end just as in regular ping-pong, but after he serves it, he puts the bat down on the table (with the handle sticking over the edge) and gets in the line to his left. The next person in line (to the server's right) picks up the bat and waits for the ball to be returned. The line keeps rotating around the table in a clockwise fashion, with each person hitting the ball once from whichever end of the table he happens to be. If he drops the bat, misses the ball, or hits it off the table, he is eliminated. When it gets down to the last two people, they must hit the ball, put the bat down, turn around, then pick up the bat, and hit the ball. Last one remaining wins.

CATEGORIES (*For C-Groups*)
This game is played exactly like rhythm. But instead of having numbers, you follow the category . . . whatever the person ahead of you called out.

To begin, everyone (a) slaps their knees and (b) claps their hands. Then, when you snap your right fingers and then your left fingers, the leader says 'cate-gory' (in two syllables).

Then the next person in the group

(going clockwise) calls out a particular 'cate—gory', such as 'vege—tables' or 'makes—of car' or 'film—stars' or 'rock—singers.'

Then, *without breaking the rhythm:* (a) slap, (b) clap, etc. . . . the next person (going clockwise) must call out something within this 'cate—gory,' such as (for 'makes—of car') 'Range—Rover' or 'Dat—sun' or 'Maes—tro'.

If you cannot think of something in the 'cate—gory' when it comes to your turn, you can change the 'cate—gory' by calling out 'cate—gory.' And the next person in the group must change the 'cate—gory' to something else WITHOUT BREAKING THE RHYTHM, such as 'football players'. And the next person must come up with a football player in this NEW 'cate—gory' without breaking the rhythm, etc.

The object of the game is to keep the rhythm. The group that keeps the rhythm the longest is the winner.

Before you start, give everyone a moment of silence to think of a 'cate—gory' in case the person ahead calls out the word 'cate—gory' and he/she has to come up with a new 'cate—gory'.

To start off all groups at the same time, the overall leader calls out . . . one . . . two . . . three . . . GO.

LEADERS' CHECKLIST

BEFORE THE SESSION

☐ Student Books: Do you have enough?

☐ Meal: Is someone preparing the food?

☐ Absentees: Ask C-Group leaders to contact anyone who was absent from their group at the last meeting.

☐ Team Training: Go over the session plan with your YWT.

☐ Crowd Breakers: Choose one or two and find the necessary equipment.

☐ TV Programmes: For the Warm-Up collect some old *TV Times* and *Radio Times.*

DURING THE SESSION

☐ Welcome: Welcome newcomers. Give them Student Books. Write in their names. Assign to a C-Group before the Warm-Up.

☐ Modelling: Share some of your own answers before asking the groups to share. Set the pace for openness.

☐ Partners: Note that C-Groups always work in pairs before discussion.

AFTER THE SESSION

☐ Collect: Collect the books unless you are assigning the Further study as homework.

☐ Reorder: Order more books for newcomers.

☐ Team Training: Get together with YWT for personal support and strategy planning. Think about an overnight retreat at the end of the course.

Session 4
Controlling the Tongue

Objectives: To continue to get better acquainted; to check, and report on, their 'mind renewal plan' from Session 3; to realise the tremendous potential of the tongue for good or for evil; to evaluate personal speech patterns; to determine a plan for improving speech habits; to continue to build a learning, sharing, caring community.

Time: From 50 minutes to 2½ hours

- ☐ Meal/30–40 Minutes*
- ☐ Crowd Breakers/25–30 Minutes*
- ☐ C-Group Warm-Up/12–15 Minutes
- ☐ Starter Bible Study/35–40 Minutes
- ☐ Going Further/25–30 Minutes*
- *Optional

If you have only 50 minutes, move to the C-Group Warm-Up immediately. If you have 2½ hours, the Further study can be incorporated into the regular meeting time. If not, you can assign this as homework for those interested in pursuing the subject. For an older, or more mature group, you can condense the time required for the Starter Bible Study and spend more time on the Further study.

Materials required:

- ☐ Student Books
- ☐ Pens
- ☐ Equipment for Crowd Breakers

Leadership: Note the 'Leaders' Checklist'.

Meal: Ask a mum or dad to prepare an inexpensive but filling hot meal and ask everyone to bring a specified sum of money to cover expenses.

Crowd Breakers: Select one or two and bring the extra equipment that is needed.

Review: If you assigned the Further study as homework, take a moment to ask how it went.

WARM-UP
C-Groups/12–15 Minutes

Hot Seat

WELCOME the group.
DISTRIBUTE the books and ASK them to turn to Session 4.

JOT DOWN (in silence) the first thing that comes to mind for each half-finished sentence. (Give an example here for one or two.) Then, GET TOGETHER in C-Groups for sharing.

APPOINT one person in each C-Group to sit in the 'hot seat'. This is simply a term for the time when all attention will be focused on this person. When a person is in the hot seat, every other person in their C-Group will guess how the hot seat person would respond to each half-finished sentence. When each person has guessed what the person in the 'hot seat' would say or do, HAVE this person explain what they jotted down in their book.

Then, ASK the next person in the group to sit in silence while the others focus on this person, etc. . . . until everyone has been in the 'hot seat'.

After the 'hot seat' is completed, ASK each person to jot down one thing they learned from this experience. Then, go around and SHARE.

STARTER BIBLE STUDY
C-Groups/35–40 Minutes

Tongue: Tamed or Troublesome?

BEGIN the study by asking the group members to report on their 'Mind Renewal Plan' from session 3. How have they been doing? What have they learned?

(Preparation, 15–20 Minutes) MOVE to the Starter Bible Study. SAY something like this, ' "Sticks and stones may break my bones, but words can never hurt me." In spite of this old rhyme, most of us know that words can be life-changing. They can destroy or heal, hurt or help. Cuts, scrapes and broken bones heal with time, but wounds caused by words often last a lifetime. James, one of the pastors of the early church in Jerusalem, wrote to young Christians about this problem.' ASK the person you've selected in advance to read the Bible passage. GET TOGETHER with someone from their C-Group (not the same person every time) and work together on the questions under 'Looking into the Story'. Then, work solo on the 'My Own Story' questions. ENCOURAGE them to be very honest and open in their evaluations.

Note: As this course progresses, more is required of the students in the 'My Own Story' section. CHALLENGE them to work and give it their best shot.

(Discussion, 20–25 Minutes) REGROUP in C-Groups for discussion. On the 'Looking into the Story' questions, HELP each person understand the tremendous potential for good and for evil of the tongue. When you emerge from these questions, everyone should realise that tongue control is crucial.

On the 'My Own Story' questions, don't force anyone in the group to share. The nature of these questions is such that they must volunteer their answers. PROBE gently, however, and encourage them—after four weeks together— to share openly what they think about their speech patterns. HAVE them share with their partners the three steps they will take this week and ASK the partners to check with each other in the middle of the week to see what progress is being made.

CLOSE in prayer. If your group seems ready, open it up to conversational prayer (short, one-sentence prayers from everyone who wishes to pray aloud) and ENCOURAGE members to pray for one another.

GOING FURTHER
C-Groups/25–30 Minutes

Tongue: Trained or Terrible?

If you have time, ASK partners to get together again and work on all questions except the Personal Application—which each person should answer individually. Then, REGATHER for discussion. This particular Further study can easily be assigned as homework.

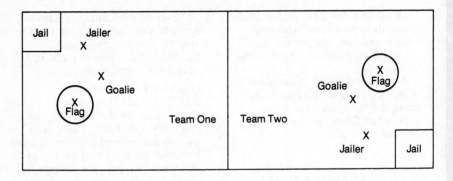

Optional Crowd Breakers

CAPTURE THE FLAG (*For two teams*)
Team 1 is on one side of the field, and Team 2 is on the other side. The idea of the game is somehow to capture the flag, located in the other team's territory, without getting tagged (or tackled, clobbered, etc.). Once you cross over the line in the middle of the field, you can be tagged, and sent to 'jail', which is set up behind each team back by the flag. However, if you are in jail, one of your team-mates can free you by getting to the jail without getting tagged, and then he can tag you, which frees you. You both get a free run back to safety. Each team has one 'goalie' who watches the flag from a distance of about ten feet away, and also a 'jailer', who guards the jail. The idea is to work out some strategy with your teammates to capture the flag.

The playing field needs to look like the one above.

PERSONAL SCAVENGER HUNT
In this scavenger hunt each C-Group is to find the item you call out and bring it to the centre. Each C-Group appoints a captain who is responsible for getting the item to the centre of the room. Start off by awarding one point for the first round . . . and double the points each round . . . so that the more difficult items get more points: For instance:

- ☐ For 1 point: A picture of the Queen (coin, note or stamp)
- ☐ For 2 points: A second-class stamp—used
- ☐ For 4 points: A sock with a hole in it
- ☐ For 8 points: 4 different-colour hairs—tied end to end
- ☐ For 16 points: A love letter
- ☐ For 32 points: One boy dressed with 4 shirts and 8 socks
- ☐ For 64 points: The entire C-Group enclosed in a rope of socks tied together

For even more points, you may want to add more impossible tasks, such as: Your C-Group leader carried bodily to the centre; two people in one shirt; one person with everyone's socks, belts, and watches, etc.

CHUBBY BUNNY

This is a marshmallow-eating contest. Ask one person from each C-Group to enter the contest. The object is to see how many marshmallows one can stuff into his or her mouth and still say 'chubby bunny'. Then, keep adding and asking them to repeat 'chubby bunny' until someone is the winner. THE RECORD is 27 marshmallows. See if you can get someone to beat this.

SCRABBLE

Here is a new way to play this game. Each C-Group is a team and given a portion of the room to spell words by quickly lying on the floor in the correct spelling of a word. BEGIN with a letter of the alphabet, such as 'O' or 'A'. Then, move on to two-letter words, such as 'AT' or 'AS'. Finally, if you have enough people in each C-Group, attempt some three-letter words, such as 'DRY' or 'ROT'. You need a large room for this game and a stepladder so that you can see from overhead. The team to spell the word correctly—lying on the floor—WINS.

DUM DUM

Slap your knees twice as you say the words: *Dum Dum*. Then grab your nose with your left hand and your left ear with your right hand while you say: *Diddy Diddy*. Slap your knees twice again to the words: *Dum Dum*. Now grab your nose with your right hand and your right ear with your left hand while you say: *Da Da*. Go faster and faster. *Dum Dum Diddy Diddy Dum Dum Da Da. Dum Dum Diddy Diddy Dum Dum Da Da,* etc.

LEADERS' CHECKLIST

BEFORE THE SESSION

□ Student Books: Have enough.

□ Meal: Ask someone to prepare the hot meal.

□ Crowd Breakers: Choose one or two and collect the equipment.

□ Absentees: Ask the C-Group leaders to contact any member of their group who was absent last week.

□ Team Training: Get together for support and go over the Bible study.

DURING THE SESSION

□ Welcome: Welcome newcomers. Give them Student Books and assign to a C-Group.

□ Warm-Up: Note the switch in sharing approach. One person at a time sits in silence while the others guess what this person has jotted down. Then, this person shares.

□ Modelling: C-Group leaders 'go first' on sharing and set the pace for others to be open.

AFTER THE SESSION

□ Collect: Collect the Student Books

□ Reorder: Order more if necessary.

□ Team: Get together, evaluate the session, and think about an overnight retreat for all the group at the end of the course.

Session 5
Sex, Sex, and More Sex

Objectives: To continue to build a learning, loving, caring, sharing community; to feel good about sex and the body; to know and understand why sex is a good gift from God and why sexual intercourse is reserved for marriage; to realise how God views sex outside of marriage; to know the source of victory over sexual temptation; to meet and question an expert on sexuality (optional).

Time: From 50 to 2½ hours

- ☐ Meal/30–40 Minutes*
- ☐ Crowd Breakers/25–30 Minutes*
- ☐ C-Group Warm-Up/7–10 Minutes
- ☐ Starter Bible Study/35–40 Minutes
- ☐ Going Further/25–30 Minutes*
- ☐ 'And Now a Word from the Experts'/30–35 Minutes*

*Optional

If you have only 50 minutes, move to the C-Group Warm-Up immediately. If you have 2½ hours, the Further study can be incorporated into the regular meeting time. If not, you can assign this as homework for those interested in pursuing the subject further. For an older, or more mature group, you can condense the time required for the Starter Bible Study and spend more time on the Further study as a group.

Materials required:
- ☐ Student Books
- ☐ Pens
- ☐ Flip chart, overhead projector or blackboard
- ☐ Equipment for Crowd Breakers

- ☐ An expert on sex—medical doctor or nurse (if you elect to use the optional suggestion)

Leadership: Continue meeting with your Youth Worker Team and C-Group Leaders to support one another and go over the session plan before each youth meeting. Also, study the 'Leaders' Checklist'.

IN ADDITION, give some special time in preparation for this session. Everyone in this age-group is interested in the subject but not everyone is able to talk about it. Because it's such a special topic, it needs special treatment. Don't treat it lightly. Don't make fun of it or the bodies of any age-group. On the other hand, don't be too heavy or too prudish. Ask God to give you the right approach and the right attitude.

You will notice that the session is designed differently from the past. The Warm-Up is longer and more serious. There is no 'Looking into the Story' separate from 'My Own Story'.

In addition, you have an opportunity to bring in an expert on sex. If possible, make this happen. It will be very beneficial for the group. If you can't make it happen on the same day as this session, schedule it for a special meeting, or next week bring in the expert and put off Session 6 for another week.

Meal: Ask one of the parents to prepare an inexpensive hot meal and ask everyone to bring an appropriate sum of money.

Crowd Breakers: Choose one or two to open the meeting. Some are for the whole group and some are for the small C-Groups.

Review: If you assigned the Further study for homework, take a few moments to ask what your group got out of their study.

**WARM-UP
C-Groups/7–10
Minutes**

Ten Questions on Sex

WELCOME the group. ASK everyone to turn in their Student Books to Session 5. Simply MENTION that today's topic is on sex (and you'll have their attention immediately!)

HAVE everyone answer the ten questions in their Student Books. Then, GET TOGETHER in C-Groups and share their answers. TAKE one question at a time and ASK for a show of hands for 'Yes' . . . 'No' . . . and '?.' When there is a difference of opinion, ask for anyone who wishes to explain their position. DON'T try to change anyone's opinion or make anyone feel that their position is unbiblical. LET THE BIBLE SPEAK FOR ITSELF when the time comes.

**STARTER BIBLE
STUDY
C-Groups/35–40
Minutes**

About Me and God's Good Gift

(Preparation/Part 1; 4–6 Minutes) ASK the C-Groups to get into twos. READ the two Bible passages aloud to the group; ASK partners to find the answers in the passages and CIRCLE the words in the puzzle.

(Give an example.) After 4 to 6 minutes, call time and move on to Part 2.

(Preparation/Part 2; 12–14 Minutes) READ the next selection of Bible verses (and the introduction) and have the group members work with their partners on the rest of the questions—including the section 'Good News'. That will probably take 12–14 minutes.

(Discussion, 15–20 Minutes) REGROUP in C-Groups and DISCUSS. COVER all the questions. Major points to discuss: Sex is a good gift from God reserved for marriage. But God understands what we are going through because he knows us and *lives within us*. He has also made it possible for us to be victors over sexual temptation and has given us a process for forgiveness when we've failed.

Then GO through these concluding statements and ASK everyone to vote yes or no on each statement. After they vote, DISCUSS why they voted as they did.

I THINK THE BIBLE SAYS THAT THE BODY:

Y	N	
□	□	was created by God and declared good by him
□	□	is only a temporary dwelling place for the soul
□	□	belongs to God
□	□	is the source of many temptations
□	□	includes a spiritual as well as a physical dimension.

I THINK THE BIBLE TEACHES THAT:

Y	N	
□	□	sexual urges are sinful
□	□	people are better off if they avoid sex
□	□	sexuality is a gift from God

☐ ☐ **sexual intercourse is limited to married couples**

☐ ☐ **abuse of one's sexuality is sinful**

Make sure they understand God's view of sex.

CLOSE in prayer. MAKE this a time of silence and meditation. ENCOURAGE the young people to talk to God silently about their sexual feelings, successes, and failures. REMIND them that they can silently confess their sins if they've failed and God will forgive them. Before you conclude with a prayer for the whole group, ask them—with their eyes closed—if anyone would like to meet with you to talk about this subject further. If they do, they can raise their hands and you'll talk to them later. Then ARRANGE TO MEET UP with those who raised their hands. This is a volatile issue and teenagers need help and understanding. (You may like to refer to the section on counselling in *Six Training Sessions for your Youth Worker Team.*)

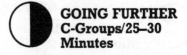 **GOING FURTHER C-Groups/25–30 Minutes**

Love and Sex

If you have time for the Further study, DON'T do it. Instead, USE this time for 'And Now a Word from the Experts.' ASSIGN the Further study as homework.

Optional Exercise 'And Now a Word from the Experts

Activity: Invite a Christian doctor and nurse, or perhaps a social worker, to come and share information and answer questions regarding the physical and emotional aspects of sexuality.

Time: About 35–40 minutes—25 minutes for presentation and 10–15 minutes for questions (but don't cut the discussion off if the group is responding well).

Materials required:

☐ Two rooms (one for the boys' discussion group, one for the girls')

☐ Paper and pens for anonymous questions

☐ Blackboard, overhead projector, chart stand, or any equipment requested by the speakers

Rationale: This activity will help your students become more comfortable with their sexuality by:

1. Giving them accurate information about the sexual changes that are occurring in their bodies.

2. Demonstrating that their sexuality is a gift from God and that Christians can discuss it with God's blessing.

3. Giving them a chance to ask questions they may have without fear of being laughed at or disapproved of.

4. Giving them the proper terminology.

INSTRUCTIONS:

1. Carefully choose a Christian doctor and nurse or other competent person who will be willing to share the biological facts of life accurately, simply, and straightforwardly. These people should be willing and capable to answer questions without making the students feel stupid or ashamed for asking. Try to spend some time with these people ahead of time to discuss what they might like to include in their presentations.

2. At the beginning of the session, introduce the topic and the guest speakers. The group members will probably feel more comfortable in separate groups for the boys and girls.

3. Distribute pens and paper and give the students a chance to write down any questions they would like to address anonymously to the experts (guest speakers).

Optional Crowd Breakers

ALL WASHED UP

For this game you need several squirt guns and candles. Have the group form pairs. One person holds the lighted candle in his mouth. His partner, across the room, tries to put the candle out with the squirt gun. Winner is the one who puts the candle out first. Be sure then to switch positions and give the other person a chance to get his face washed too.

HEADS

Divide the group in half, each on one side of the room. Each person grabs a partner from his side of the room. One of the pair sits in a chair with a paper cup on top of his head. The other person tries to knock the paper cup off those across the room by throwing marshmallows, standing behind his partner. The winner is the pair who keeps their paper cup on the longest.

SARDINE TAG

One who is 'it' hides while the group counts to 100 with eyes closed. Then everyone goes to look for 'it.' When they find 'it' they get in, wherever 'it' is, trying not to let anyone else see. The last person to find the group is 'it' next time.

PAPER AEROPLANE CONTEST

Everyone makes their own paper aeroplane. While they are doing that, put a large dartboard in the middle of the room. The inside circle is worth 20 points, middle circle 10, and the outside circle is worth 5. Each person gets a chance to throw his/her aeroplane three times. The one with the most points wins.

LEADERS' CHECKLIST

BEFORE THE SESSION

- ☐ Outside Expert: If you decide to go with the Optional Exercise—'And Now a Word from the Experts'— contact this person(s) and brief him/ her on what you want.

- ☐ Absentees: Ask the C-Group leaders to contact those who were absent last week.

- ☐ Crowd Breakers: Choose one or two and get your team members to collect the necessary equipment.

- ☐ Team Training: Continue meeting as a support group and go over the session plan together.

DURING THE SESSION

- ☐ Welcome: Welcome newcomers. Give them Student Books and assign them to a C-Group.

- ☐ Introduction: Introduce the topic of sex properly. Re-read the suggestions under 'leadership'.

- ☐ Starter Bible Study: Note that the Bible teaching is in two parts.

- ☐ Prayer: Note that the prayer time is in silence, followed by an opportunity for anyone who wants to talk with you privately to raise their hand. Follow up on this with great care.

- ☐ Outside Expert: If you have invited an outside person(s) to answer questions about sex, make sure you give enough time for this experience.

AFTER THE SESSION

- ☐ Collect: Collect the Student Books unless you are assigning the Further study as homework.

- ☐ Follow up: Follow up any in your Group who indicated a need to talk further about sex. You may find it helpful to read over the principles of counselling in the Youth Worker Training book.

Session 6

Honesty and Integrity

Objectives: To continue to develop the C-Group into a loving, caring, sharing unit; to understand what the Bible means by honesty and integrity; to realise that honesty and integrity are two characteristics valued highly by God and important to maturity; to evaluate your own honesty and integrity; and to develop a plan to live more honestly.

Time: From 50 minutes to 2½ hours

- ☐ Meal/30–40 Minutes*
- ☐ Crowd Breakers/25–30 Minutes*
- ☐ C-Group Warm-Up/10–12 Minutes
- ☐ Starter Bible Study/35–40 Minutes
- ☐ Going Further/25–30 Minutes*

*Optional

If you have only 50 minutes, move to the C-Group Warm-Up immediately. If you have 2½ hours, the Further study can be incorporated into the regular meeting time. If not, you can assign this as homework for those interested in pursuing the subject further. For an older, or more mature group, you can condense the time required for the Starter Bible Study and spend more time on the Further study.

Materials required:

- ☐ Student Books
- ☐ Pens
- ☐ Equipment for Crowd Breakers

Leadership: Meet once a week with your C-Group leaders for support and planning. Study the 'Leaders' Checklist'.

Meal: If you're planning a meal, make sure you've contacted a mum or dad to bring the food and that you've told everyone how much money they need to bring.

Crowd Breakers: Choose one or two and assign team members to bring the necessary equipment.

Review: If you assigned the Further study for homework, take a few minutes to ask what they got out of their study.

WARM-UP
C-Groups/10–15 Minutes

Lines of Extremes

WELCOME your friends. DISTRIBUTE the books. ASK them to turn to Session 6.

(Preparation, 5–7 Minutes) EXPLAIN that there are two parts to the Warm-Up. They are to complete both parts in silence. (Give an example of where you would put an 'x' on the first line . . . and what you would circle in the second exercise.)

(*Discussion, 5–7 Minutes*) GET TOGETHER in C-Groups. HAVE one person at a time share where they placed their 'x' on the lines and what they circled in the second series. Then, ASK the others in the C-Group if they agree with this person's self-appraisal.

GIVE each person a chance to share their responses and the others in the C-Group a chance to respond. NOTE: This will give you some understanding of how individuals feel about themselves when it comes to honesty and integrity.

STARTER BIBLE STUDY
C-Groups/35–40 Minutes

Wise Up

(*Preparation 20–25 Minutes*) ASK the person you've selected in advance to read the introduction and the Bible passage. Then, INSTRUCT the C-Groups to form pairs and work together on questions 1–4 under 'Looking into the Story'. The fill-in-the-blank questions will require some effort, so ENCOURAGE them to give it their best shot together. This could take close to 15 minutes. DON'T let them get bogged down.

BREAK IN and ASK everyone to move on to the 'My Own Story' section and work on their own. Plan on another 7–10 minutes for this.

(*Discussion, 15–20 Minutes*) CALL the C-Groups back together. In the discussion, CONCENTRATE first on what the words and statements mean in the Proverbs text. THE POINT: God values integrity and honesty highly and he wants us to value and practise these qualities.

In question 2 of 'My Own Story', REFLECT on some of the statements and ask the group where their answers differed from how God would probably have answered and why they had these differences. Then, GO through the remaining questions.

CLOSE in prayer, ENCOURAGING members of the C-Group to pray for one another. CHALLENGE them to help each other this week at school/college/work, in the neighbourhood, or through phone conversations to live a life of integrity and honesty.

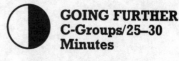

GOING FURTHER
C-Groups/25–30 Minutes

Steps to Honesty

If you have time, DO the Further study. INSTRUCT the C-Groups to work on questions 1–3 in pairs, and 4, 5 and the Personal Application alone. REGATHER for discussion. HELP each person develop a plan for this particular area expressed in the prayer. Do this by asking volunteers to share their area(s) of growth and by brainstorming as a group on how that person could succeed.

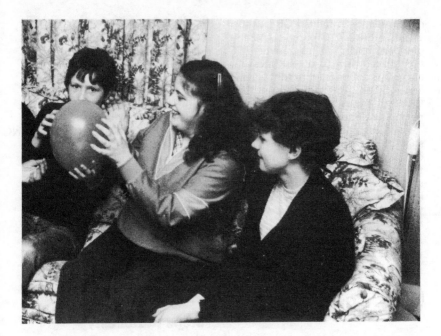

Optional Crowd Breakers

THIS IS A CUP! A WHAT?
In your C-Groups, pass two objects around your group at the same time in *opposite* directions.

☐ A pretty paper cup
☐ A round rubber balloon

On the word GO, the person holding the two objects turns to the person on the right, hands this person the cup, and says, *'This is a pretty paper cup.'* The person on the right replies: 'A what?' And the first person answers: 'A pretty paper cup!'

Then the second person hands the cup to the person on the right and says: 'This is a pretty paper cup!' The third person replies: 'A what?' The second person, in turn, asks the first person, 'A what?' And the first person answers the second person, 'A pretty paper cup' . . . and the second person answers to the third person, 'A pretty paper cup,' etc. . . .

Now, while the 'pretty paper cup' is going in the right direction, the first person starts the 'round rubber balloon' in the left direction by saying to the person on the left, 'This is a round rubber balloon.' And the second person on the left responds, 'A what?' And the first person answers, 'A round rubber balloon.'

In other words, the response 'A what?' must come back to the first person *each* time . . . and the answer, 'A pretty paper cup' . . . or 'round rubber balloon' must be repeated back *each* time down the line.

When the balloon has gone all the way around the group, the last person in the group should sit on it . . . until it pops.

On the word GO, the person holding the two objects starts the 'pretty paper cup' to the right . . . and the 'round rubber balloon' to the left. And each time, the 'A what?' must come all the way back to the first person.

SCULPTURING

Get together in C-Groups and form pairs. One person is modelling clay and the other person is the artist/sculptor.

Round 1: The leader calls out a word and the artist in the twosome has 10 seconds to mould his/her partner into this word. Then the leader will scream 'Freeze', and the person who is the modelling clay must 'freeze' in the position they are in. (Leader: start out with some easy feelings such as: fear . . . joy . . . tension . . . rejection.)

Round 2: Get together in fours: Two people are modelling clay and the other two are the artists. The leader now calls out relational words and gives the two artists/sculptors 10 seconds to mould their 'modelling clay' into these relationships. Then the leader screams 'Freeze' and the modelling clay people 'freeze' as a statue in this relationship. (Here are some relational words to call out: trust . . . distrust . . . confrontation . . . reassurance.)

Round 3: Get the entire C-Group together. This time, everyone is modelling clay, as well as the artist/ sculptor. Somehow, you must quickly decide on the meaning of the word and sculpt yourselves into this word. You will have 30 seconds. Then the leader will scream 'Freeze' and you are to freeze in position. (Leader: start off with something like . . . 'game of volley ball'. Yell 'Freeze' and comment on their sculptures. Then call out . . . 'Christian community' and give them 30 seconds to sculpt what this means.)

LEADERS' CHECKLIST

BEFORE THE SESSION

☐ Student Books: If you asked the members of the group to do the Further study as homework, contact them to make sure they bring their books back.

☐ Meal: Check arrangements with the parent you asked to prepare the hot meal.

☐ Absentees: Ask the C-Group leaders to call their absentees.

☐ Team: Get together with your C-Group leaders and go over the session plan.

☐ Crowd Breakers: Choose one or two and ask team members to bring the special equipment.

DURING THE SESSION

☐ Welcome: Welcome newcomers. Assign them to a C-Group.

☐ Demonstrate: For the Warm-Up, demonstrate how the sharing is done—with one person explaining their own markings and letting the group 'affirm' what they reported.

☐ Model: In the Starter Bible Study, take a moment and explain your own answers to set the mood for honesty and openness.

☐ Going Further: The material is a little harder and needs a little encouragement from the C-Group leaders.

AFTER THE SESSION

☐ Celebration: Plan something special at the next session to conclude the course.

☐ Plan: Select another course to start on after a few weeks of rest.

☐ Team: Think about recruiting some more people for your Youth Worker Team for the next course.

Session 7

Forgiveness: The Key to Moving On

Objectives: To complete the course successfully, to *be* a loving, caring, sharing community for one another; to evaluate personally what progress has been made during the course; to understand the liberating power of forgiveness and to experience forgiveness personally and move on with Christ, regardless of what has happened in the past.

Time: From 50 minutes to 2½ hours

- ☐ Meal/30–40 Minutes*
- ☐ C-Group Warm-Up/12–15 Minutes
- ☐ Starter Bible Study/30–35 Minutes
- ☐ Going Further/25–30 Minutes*
- ☐ Worship Service or Party/Open-ended*

*Optional

If you have only 50 minutes, move to the C-Group Warm-Up immediately. If you have 2½ hours, think about a special close for this course with a worship experience or party.

Materials required:

- ☐ Student Books
- ☐ Pens
- ☐ One piece of paper per student for the Further study.
- ☐ If you are planning a special celebration at the close, bring the supplies

Leadership: If you do not have time to do the Further study as a group, review the material so that you can summarise it as part of the Starter Bible Study. Also, think about closing this course with a special worship experience or party.

Meal: If you're planning a meal, make sure that you've contacted a parent about the meal and the group members about bringing money to cover the cost.

Review: If you assigned the Further study last week for homework, take a few minutes to let your Group share what they learned.

 WARM-UP C-Groups/12–15 Minutes

Moments

WELCOME the troops. BEFORE they do the Warm-Up, ASK everyone to turn to the front of their books, 'Here's Where I Am', and retake the exercise. (If you did not use this exercise in the first session, don't worry about it. Do the exercise anyway). ASK them to put an 'x' where they are now and then to write at the bottom of the page how they have changed since they first took this exercise. HOLD the sharing on this exercise for a moment.

ASK everyone to turn to Session 7 and to work alone on the Warm-Up exercise—'Moments.' (Share a couple of 'moments' in your experience to demonstrate what is meant.) NOTE: This is a more personal, slightly heavier Warm-Up than normal. But now the group has been together for 7 weeks, the members should be able to share some of these moments from their lives.

GET TOGETHER in C-Groups. BEGIN by looking at the 'Here's Where I Am' exercise. ASK your Group members to explain where they have changed.

Then, MOVE to the Warm-Up and let each person share any *two moments*—one that is funny and one that is serious.

STARTER BIBLE STUDY
C-Groups/30–35 Minutes

The Runaway

(Preparation, 5–8 Minutes) ASK a couple of people this week to read the Bible passage. It is a bit longer and your two readers can alternate paragraphs for variety. Again, ASK them to work in pairs on the 'Looking into the Story' section and solo on the 'My Own Story' questions. The questions should take about 5–8 minutes.

(Discussion, 25–30 Minutes) REGATHER in C-Groups and DISCUSS all of the questions. HELP them really to understand the plight of the runaway and the unconditional forgiveness of the father. MOVE through the 'My Own Story' questions, concentrating on 4 and 5. *If you do not have time for the Further study, take 3 or 4 minutes at the close of the Starter Bible Study and summarise the content of the Further study. The goal is to help each student understand and experience God's loving forgiveness regardless of where or how they may have failed in the past.

CLOSE in prayer thanking God for the group; for the 7 weeks together and for the liberating power of his forgiveness.

GOING FURTHER
C-Groups/25–30 Minutes

Forgiveness as a Way of Life

This is a critical part of the study. An understanding of forgiveness as 'a way of life' and experiencing God's grace is so important in the Christian life. HAVE them work with their partner on everything but the Personal Application. They should work solo on that. (DISTRIBUTE a sheet of paper to each person for this.)

REGATHER and DISCUSS this important truth together.

CLOSING
All Together/Open-ended

To celebrate your experience during this course, here are two options:

Quaker Service: This is sometimes called a 'testimonial' meeting.

Move to a quiet, meditative place, such as the chancel in the church . . . or turn out the lights and light a fire . . . or candles. Begin the service by explaining a little about the Quaker tradition and the importance of being in silence . . . letting God speak to us before we speak to him or to others.

To introduce the period of silence, lead the group in singing together a meditative hymn or chorus to focus the attention. Then wait in silence until someone breaks the silence with their sharing.

Suggest that the sharing be limited to the 'next steps' in their spiritual journey . . . and where they need the support of the community in their venture.

Set the pace with your own example. Make it personal, very specific . . . and honest.

Commissioning Service. Change the atmosphere in the room or move to another place. This service is best carried out in small clusters—with people that know each other.

Give each person in the group a chance to explain the 'next step' in their life . . . or what 'God is asking me to do'. Then have this person kneel or sit in the centre of the group while the others in the group commission this person to the task they have explained, one person praying for the whole group while everyone 'lays their hands' on the head or shoulders.

Then the next person explains where they need to move out . . . and kneels in the group to be commissioned, etc., until everyone has been commissioned.